COLLECTIBLE
GLASS
SHOES

including:
Metal
Pottery
Figural &
Porcelain
Shoes

EARLENE WHEATLEY

COLLECTOR BOOKS
A Division of Schroeder Publishing Co., Inc.

The current values in this book should be used only as a guide. They are not intended to set prices, which vary from one section of the country to another. Auction prices as well as dealer prices vary greatly and are affected by condition as well as demand. Neither the Author nor the Publisher assumes responsibility for any losses that might be incurred as a result of consulting this guide.

SEARCHING FOR A PUBLISHER?

We are always looking for knowledgable people considered to be experts within their fields. If you feel that there is a real need for a book on your collectible subject and have a large comprehensive collection, contact Collector Books.

Book design by: Karen Long
Cover design by: Beth Summers

On the Cover: Row one: High heeled slipper. $25.00. **Row two:** Pale blue shoe held by an elf. $75.00. Porcelain shoe with chickens as decoration. $60.00. **Row three:** High-heeled slipper held by a pair of hands. $45.00. Burmese. $15.00 – 20.00. **Row Four:** Ruby cocktail shaker. $450.00 – 600.00. Blue and white millefiore. $35.00 – 45.00.

CONTENTS

CREDITS AND ACKNOWLEDGMENTS

Some of the glass shoe descriptions are reprinted from *Victorian Glass* by Ruth Webb Lee, by special permission from Charles E. Tuttle, Co., Inc., Rutland, Vermont. The description of the Degenhart shoes were reprinted from *Degenhart Glass and Paperweights* by special permission from the Degenhart Museum.

A special thanks to Patrick Braden for the loan of his Victorian pewter shoe on the cranberry foot; Mr. & Mrs. Keith Bartow for the lovely shoes from England; Gary Swain for inviting me to his auction where I bought the condiment slipper; Mr. Albert C. Revi for the use of some of his illustrations from *Nineteenth Century Glass: Its Genesis and Development*; Mary Witoski of the Bridgeport, Connecticut, Historical Society for her assistance in the research of the J.B. trademark; Mr. Fennmore of the Henry Frances DuPont Winterhur Museum for steering me in the right direction in my search for information on silver shoes; Mr. Samuel Hough for the research on Gorham silver shoes; the Smithsonian Institute for the copy of the Butler Bros. catalog; the librarians of Pasadena, Glendale, and Los Angeles for their assistance; Dorla Battersby of Robbins Antique Mart, who located a shoe lamp by Atterbury; Sandy Cloud, China Closet; Ralph Hickman, Inland Empire Antiques; Mike Hawkins, Showcase Antiques; Ron's Antiques and Collectibles of Pomona, California; Beth Guernsey, Long Beach, California; Georges' of Fullerton, California; Jabberwocky Antiques of San Dimas, California; Joyce and Jack Williams of Irvine, California; Sandy Hockaday; Elena Weisert; and the many dealers I did not mention, I thank you. John, who was there through the frustrations of photography, writing, re-writing, and assembly of the manuscript. My family, whose love I have, my tribute, I will use the family name Wheatley. Debby Hughes, my typist, who made it all happen by deciphering my handwriting and tolerating the many, many re-writes, she never lost her patience.

A debt of gratitude and acknowledgment to A.G. Peterson for his work on glass patents and his willingness to share. To the many authors whose work I used as references, I appreciate and thank you for your contribution to shoe collecting.

An apology and thanks to the many dealers who located over a hundred shoes that I did not photograph.

A big thanks to Shelby Good and Kacie Carroll of *Antique Living* in Lancaster, California, for locating a shoe collection that I did not photograph.

To the publishers at Collector Books, thanks for their patience and understanding.

ABOUT THE AUTHOR

Earlene Wheatley, a registered nurse, has been a collector of miniature shoes for over twenty years. She has traveled across the United States in search of shoes for her collection. During her travels she observed the actual production of glass shoes. Earlene owned an antique business in the Los Angeles area and continues to dabble in the business by selling small antiques at the "shows." She has broadened her knowledge of antiques by taking classes in the appraisal of antiques and collectibles.

She is responsible for the founding of a shoe club for collectors. Earlene is in constant search of shoes — looking for the ones she does not have.

COLLECTOR'S LAMENT

Shoe collectors share the same enthusiasm every other collector does, and this poem from a July, 1944 House and Garden appropriately fits all collectors.

I have objects perpendicular,
Ceramic and vehicular,
I've mugs and keys and butterflies and stamps,
Figurines of alabaster,
Turkish bath towels from the Astor.
I have Chippendale and Lowestoft and lamps.
I have autographs of kings,
and some prehistoric things,
I have dressing gowns of famous men who've died.
Whether fad or fashion,
I confess it is my passion,
To collect and sort the object of my pride.
I cannot stop collecting,
Although really I'm expecting
That in time I'll have to take a larger house.
In my collection numismatic
Is now filling up the attic where the only one to view it.
Is a mouse.
My wife complains my pewter
(And I can't refute her).
Leaves no shelf room for the chinaware at all
My French and English tapestry,
My early charts and mapistry
are crowding all her pictures off the wall.
I've tried to spurn collecting,
To take up vivisecting,
Or badminton, or painting, or the dance.
I've tried fielding for the Dodgers —
Then I find an old (and sworn authentic) lance
and I'm off — collecting fever in my blood.
If I were in the rain
of the overseas campaign,
In my leisure time, I'd start collecting mud.
My unfulfilled ambitions
for old prints and first editions
only complicate my plight, and I presume
If my hobbies keep on growing,
and the house starts overflowing,
My wife will have to take a furnished room

Author Unknown

INTRODUCTION

This book on collectible shoes attempts to provide information for novice collectors, and new dealers, and hopefully confirm or enhance the knowledge of the experienced collectors. "Always buy carefully" is an expression or advice that is meant for the new collectors as they begin or as they add to their collection.

I began collecting shoes in 1968, not with a purchase, but with a gift of a glass shoe from an aunt, now deceased. It was after her death that I bought the second shoe, which started my collection. With limited knowledge, locating shoes to buy became an obsession. This obsession caused me to make some mistakes because I bought shoes compulsively and paid high prices. I learned from my mistakes and gained knowledge.

My interest heightened as antique shoes became more difficult to locate. I was given a copy of a first edition of Ruth Webb Lee's book, *Victorian Glass*, where she devoted a chapter on shoes/slippers. It was her book that aroused my curiosity to seek more information about porcelain shoes as well as the glass. What I discovered as I continued my search was fragmented information from several books and undocumented statements from other collectors.

Shoe collecting is fascinating and fun. Over the years, I searched and hunted for shoes in every town I visited. During my travels, I met collectors with small collections of less than one hundred shoes and several collectors with more than five hundred. Every collector has some interesting stories to tell, the novice collector as well as the experienced.

Collectible Glass Shoes became an idea after many years of collecting, seeking information, and seeing other collections. The assembly and preparation of the manuscript became a goal that sometimes appeared unattainable. What is shared with the readers is years of research.

When you read or glance through this book, keep an open mind and accept the fact that not all of your questions will be answered. We may disagree; I certainly have disagreed with some authors, and now they can disagree with me. There will always be different opinions and there will never be only one person who knows everything about a subject. It will be great to have the reader's comments; I look forward to hearing from you.

Earlene Wheatley
P.O. Box 2390
Apple Valley, CA 92308

SHOE COLLECTING

Shoe collecting became popular during the Victorian era (1840–1890) because of the added affluence brought on by the Industrial Revolution. To the Victorians, magnificence and wealth meant quantities of decorative objects, and shoes were one of the choice objects of the ladies. According to Albert C. Revi in his book, *American Pressed Glass and Figure Bottles*, glass shoes were popular as novelty items in the mid-1800s in America. Several glassmakers and designers obtained patents to produce shoes.

In 1876, the first centennial of the independence of the United States was held in Philadelphia. Gillinder and Sons set up an exhibition factory and sales office on the Centennial Exposition grounds. Visitors saw how glass was made, and purchased small shoes that were marked "Gillinder & Sons, Centennial Exposition 1876."

The Victorians can be credited for keeping shoe collecting in the forefront. Tiny shoes were an esteemed symbol of Victoriana and appeared on everything from gifts to greeting cards. They were used as tiny bouquet holders, snuff boxes, trinket holders, toothpick holders, salt cellars, pin cushions, and as match holders. Once America became a fully industrialized country, the need for these small shoes as utility objects diminished. Shoe collecting has survived partly because the utilitarian focus changed to the decorative focus.

Shoe collectors are lured by shoes or slippers produced during the 1800s and early 1900s that were made of glass or porcelain. These serious collectors consider beauty and quality to be the requisites in addition to the age. Slippers and shoes that were produced for events such as expositions and fairs have historical significance and are sought by some collectors as a specialty.

Americans depended on the European countries for the novelty items such as shoes during the Victorian era, and some were brought back by visiting tourists. The habit of collecting mementos of travel abroad during the early nineteenth century was well established, and small slippers, marked "a present from…" followed by the name of the country, were found and bought. The first occasion for souvenirs in England was probably in 1851 when over six million people traveled to London to visit the Great Exhibition. Hordes of Americans returned home with slippers and shoes from their trip.

It was Germany that best fulfilled the need for cheap small souvenirs such as shoes. From about 1880, porcelain factories in Bavaria, Austria, and Czechoslovakia produced shoes and slippers that were exported to Britain and bought by travelers who gave them to friends and placed some on the shelves of their cabinets. (Imports to the United States flourished up to 1918 when World War I stopped the flow.)

A new collector should not become discouraged when searching for antique shoes, because they are out there. Searching in every town and antique store is the key. It appears that old glass shoes without a few nicks and chips are scarce. Collectors may be tempted to buy shoes with nicks and chips; this is acceptable *only* if they are rare and will be used to study the style of pattern and are priced accordingly. Caution: Do not consider damaged slippers or shoes as part of your collection. Do not buy chipped or nicked slippers with the idea of repairing them. The restoration of glass or pottery is a lengthy and delicate process and should be undertaken only if really necessary and by a reputable restorer. A poor repair of damage can reduce the value significantly. For this reason, many small fractures and chips are not mended. *Let the buyer beware!*

PATENT GUIDE

This guide can prove to be indispensable for anyone interested in dating antiques and collectibles through the U.S. Registered Patent System.

When an article has more than one patent number, choose the larger number.

Year	Patent #	Year	Patent #	Year	Patent #	Year	Patent #	Year	Patent #
1859	22,477	1883	269,820	1907	839,799	1931	1,787,424	1955	2,698,434
1860	26,642	1884	291,016	1908	875,679	1932	1,839,190	1956	2,728,913
1861	31,005	1885	310,168	1909	908,436	1933	1,892,663	1957	2,775,762
1862	34,045	1886	353,494	1910	945,010	1934	1,941,449	1958	2,818,567
1863	37,266	1887	355,291	1911	980,178	1935	1,985,878	1959	2,866,973
1864	41,047	1888	375,720	1912	1,013,095	1936	2,026,516	1960	2,919,443
1865	45,685	1889	395,305	1913	1,049,326	1937	2,066,309	1961	2,966,681
1866	51,784	1890	418,665	1914	1,083,267	1938	2,104,004	1962	3,015,103
1867	60,685	1891	443,987	1915	1,123,212	1939	2,142,080	1963	3,070,801
1868	72,959	1892	466,315	1916	1,166,419	1940	2,185,170	1964	3,116,487
1869	85,503	1893	488,976	1917	1,210,389	1941	2,227,418	1965	3,163,865
1870	98,460	1894	511,744	1918	1,251,458	1942	2,268,540	1966	3,226,729
1871	110,617	1895	531,619	1919	1,290,027	1943	2,307,007	1967	3,295,143
1872	122,304	1896	552,502	1920	1,329,352	1944	2,338,081	1968	3,360,800
1873	134,504	1897	574,369	1921	1,364,063	1945	2,366,154	1969	3,419,907
1874	146,120	1898	596,467	1922	1,401,948	1946	2,391,856	1970	3,487,470
1875	158,350	1899	616,871	1923	1,440,362	1947	2,413,675	1971	3,551,909
1876	171,641	1900	640,167	1924	1,478,996	1948	2,433,824	1972	3,631,539
1877	185,813	1901	664,827	1925	1,521,590	1949	2,457,797	1973	3,707,729
1878	198,733	1902	690,385	1926	1,568,040	1950	2,492,944	1974	3,781,914
1879	211,078	1903	717,521	1927	1,612,790	1951	2,536,016		
1880	223,210	1904	748,567	1928	1,654,521	1952	2,580,379		
1881	240,373	1905	778,834	1929	1,696,897	1953	2,624,046		
1882	254,836	1906	808,618	1930	1,742,181	1954	2,664,562		

POTTERY AND PORCELAIN SHOES

Both pottery and porcelain shoes have clay as a common base, but there are some fundamental differences. Pottery shoes are heavier, porous, opaque, and sometimes of colored clay. Porcelain shoes are not made of any one single clay found in nature. They are made from several selected ingredients. These ingredients are a compound of kaolin, feldspar, and silica. When this mixture of ingredients is fired to a temperature of above 2300°F or 1260°C, a shoe that is white, dense, completely vitrified, and translucent is produced. This translucence can be seen by holding the shoe up to a bright light to obscure the diffused light.

Shoes made of porcelain are divided into two categories: soft paste which is fired at a lower temperature, permeable, lightweight, slightly translucent, and requires a glaze, and hard paste which is fired at a higher temperature, vitrified, highly translucent, and does not require a glaze. George Ware, in his book *German and Austrian Porcelain*, stated that the body beneath the glaze of soft paste is easily scratched with a knife or file. Incidentally, this old idea of scratching with a knife as a test for hardness is not recommended and is unreliable. Hard paste is not easily scratched and a light tap with the ring finger and thumb or a pencil will produce a bell-like metallic ring.

A pottery shoe will break easier than a porcelain one. Porcelain is more durable and more expensive to produce than pottery.

In general, there is no rule-of-thumb method by which the beginner can distinguish between the hard and soft paste. There are important differences in their textures and usually, though not always, in their appearance. It has been stated that the enamels tend to take differently on their surfaces.

Quick recognition can only be the result of the experience gained through handling, studying, and comparing shoes of each kind of paste.

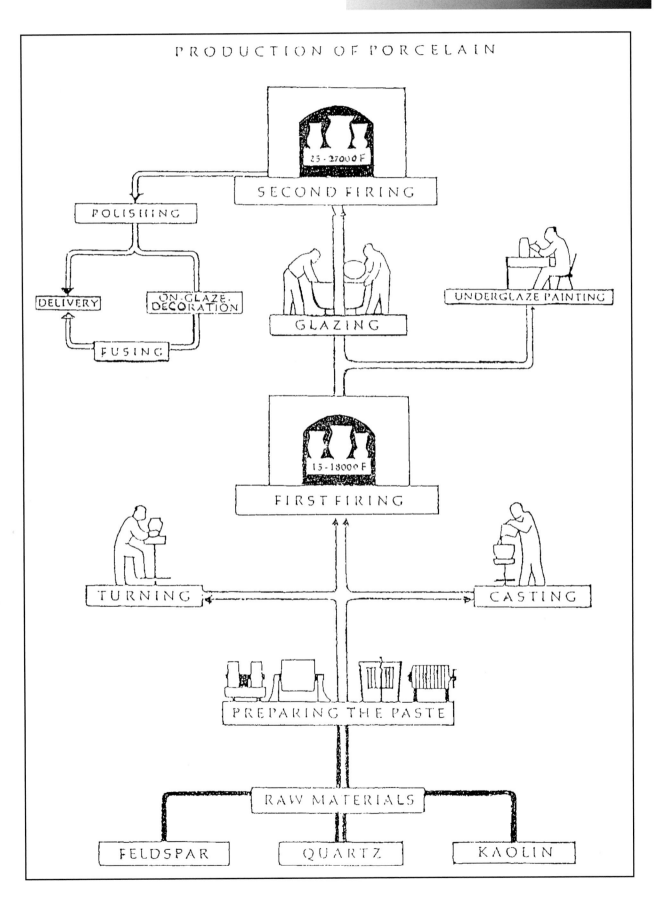

PRODUCTION OF PORCELAIN

MARKS AND PATENTS

POTTERY AND PORCELAIN MARKS

Some collectors will focus on a mark and overlook the merit of the individual shoe. A mark, however, could allow the collector the opportunity to connect the mark to a specific manufacturer or artist and may often establish the date of manufacture. Savage (1955) believed that marks should not be too strongly emphasized but should be regarded as confirmatory evidence when all other details appear to be right. Marks are an excellent clue, but not a guarantee of the origin of the slipper or shoe.

Marks must not ever be the sole criteria of excellence or even the market value. Collectors must be aware that the most fraudulent act encountered is that of faked and forged marks. The most difficult to imitate and most reliable are those under the glaze. Once marks are under the glaze, it is difficult to remove or alter them without raising suspicion.

There are two kinds of under-glaze marks, those stamped or incised on an item while the ware is soft, and those painted under the glaze. Down to the end of the eighteenth century, all under-glaze marks were in blue. It is only in the nineteenth century that under-glaze marks in black, pink, and green are found printed, not painted. According to Godden (1968), marks are applied in three ways: impressed in the soft body before firing, printed either under or over the glaze during the process of decorating, or painted by hand during or after decorating. Some authors mention a raised mark, which means the mark stands above the surface. Marks that are painted over the glaze detract greatly from the value of the shoe. It is this mark, that if an alteration is to be made, could be done by removal and replacement of a different mark.

The importance of a mark varies from one collector to another due to their sophistication and ability to recognize a well-made unmarked antique shoe. Some seasoned or sophisticated collectors realize that marks are not as old as porcelain, and will not pass up a well-made pottery or porcelain shoe because it is not marked.

Godden offers general guides for dating British porcelain or pottery marks in his book *Antique Glass and China*:

1. Printed marks incorporating the Royal Arms are nineteenth century or later.
2. Any printed mark incorporating the name of the pattern may be regarded as subsequent to 1810.
3. The use of "Limited" or abbreviations "LTD," "LD," etc. after the firm's title or initials denotes a date after 1860, and was in fact rarely used before 1880.
4. The use of the word "Royal" in the manufacturer's title or trade name suggests a date after the middle of the nineteenth century.
5. The incorporation of the words "Trade Mark" signifies a date after the Trade Mark Act of 1862.
6. The inclusion of the word "England" indicates a date after 1875, and in most cases this word was added to marks from 1891 to comply with the "American" McKinley Tariff Act, which required the country of origin to be stamped on all imported wares. The term "made in England" points to a twentieth century dating.

BRITISH REGISTRY MARKS AND PATTERN NUMBERS

One of the most useful marks for dating English porcelain and glass is the design registration mark and pattern number. Bernard Hughes, in his book *Victorian Pottery and Porcelain*, stated that until 1839, the only English law protecting industrial design was an act of 1794 giving three months copyright to designs on linens and calicoes.

The artists and manufacturers deplored their lack of protection against piracy of original creations. After an Act of Parliament in 1841, the copyright (Registration) on ceramics and glass was extended to three years. An amendment in 1842 extended protection to designs not specifically ornamental in character. All designs covered by registration were required to have the diamond-shaped mark from 1842 through 1883.

Manufacturers were divided into thirteen classes: class I, metal; class II, wood, including papier maché; class III, glass; class IV, pottery and porcelain. The others are not mentioned because shoes would not have been manufactured in those classes. The law required the marking of all protected articles with the letters "®d" (registered), together with code letters and numerals corresponding with the date of registration.

The exact date a design was registered can be decoded from the mark. Until 1867, the year was shown by the letter in the top part of the diamond, and the other three parts indicted: the left, the month of issue; the right, the day of issue; the bottom of the diamond, the parcel number or bundle. This number identifies the manufacturer. By 1868, all of the letters had been used, making it necessary to rearrange them. The top of the diamond under the new arrangement is the day of issue; left, the parcel number or bundle; right, the year; the bottom part, the month.

The diamond mark was no longer used beginning January 1884. It became a requirement that English porcelain, pottery, and glass be registered using an ®d number. This number was the equivalent to the American patent number and indicated that the design was registered at the patent office and could not be copied in any form.

If a collector owns a shoe with a registry mark or pattern number, it is worth the time to check the pattern numbers. These numbers only indicate the date at which the shoe was first put into circulation and shows with a degree of certainty that a shoe could not be earlier than the date on the shoe. A collector knows that if a shoe has a ®d number it was made after 1884.

British Registry numbers and pattern numbers can be obtained from:

The Registry Patent Office Design
25 Southhampton Building
London, WC. 2 England

REGISTRATION MARKS (1842 – 1883)

A diamond-shaped mark, printed or impressed, is often seen on wares first made between 1842 and 1883, indicating that to prevent piracy a particular design on article had been registered with the London Patent Office. It will of course be clear that the information thus given in the marks will only indicate the earliest possible date of manufacture, since the design so registered could have been continued in succeeding years.

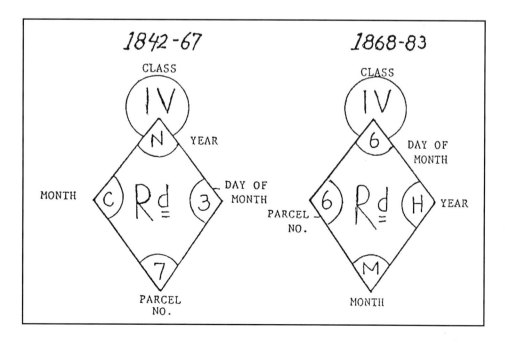

REGISTRATION MARKS AND REGISTERED PATTERNS

Index to Year and Month Letters

YEARS

1842–67 Year Letter at Top		*1868–83* Year Letter at Right	
A = 1845	N = 1864	A = 1871	L = 1882
B = 1858	O = 1862	C = 1870	P = 1877
C = 1844	P = 1851	D = 1878	S = 1875
D = 1852	Q = 1866	E = 1881	U = 1874
E = 1855	R = 1861	F = 1873	V = 1876
F = 1847	S = 1849	H = 1869	W = 1865
G = 1863	T = 1867	I = 1872	X = 1868
H = 1843	U = 1848	J = 1880	Y = 1868
I = 1846	V = 1850	K = 1883	
J = 1854	W = 1865		
K = 1857	X = 1842		
L = 1856	Y = 1853		
M = 1859	Z = 1860		

MONTHS

(Both Periods)

A = Dec.	K = Nov. & Dec. 1860
B = Oct.	M = June
C = Jan.	R = Aug. (& 1–19 Sept. 1857)
D = Sept.	
E = May	
G = Feb.	W = Mar.
H = Apr.	
I = July	

Table of Design Registration Numbers, Found on Wares from 1884

Rᵈ No.	1	Reg. in Jan. 1884
Rᵈ No.	19754	Reg. in Jan. 1885
Rᵈ No.	40480	Reg. in Jan. 1886
Rᵈ No.	64520	Reg. in Jan. 1887
Rᵈ No.	90483	Reg. in Jan. 1888
Rᵈ No.	116648	Reg. in Jan. 1889
Rᵈ No.	141273	Reg. in Jan. 1890
Rᵈ No.	163767	Reg. in Jan. 1891
Rᵈ No.	185713	Reg. in Jan. 1892
Rᵈ No.	205240	Reg. in Jan. 1893
Rᵈ No.	224720	Reg. in Jan. 1894
Rᵈ No.	246975	Reg. in Jan. 1895
Rᵈ No.	268392	Reg. in Jan. 1896
Rᵈ No.	291241	Reg. in Jan. 1897
Rᵈ No.	311658	Reg. in Jan. 1898
Rᵈ No.	331707	Reg. in Jan. 1899
Rᵈ No.	351202	Reg. in Jan. 1900
Rᵈ No.	368154	Reg. in Jan. 1901
Rᵈ No.	385500*	Reg. in Jan. 1902
Rᵈ No.	420500*	Reg. in Jan. 1903
Rᵈ No.	420000*	Reg. in Jan. 1904
Rᵈ No.	447000*	Reg. in Jan. 1905
Rᵈ No.	471000*	Reg. in Jan. 1906
Rᵈ No.	494000*	Reg. in Jan. 1907
Rᵈ No.	519500*	Reg. in Jan. 1908
Rᵈ No.	550000*	Reg. in Jan. 1909

Approximate numbers only

HEIRLOOMS OF TOMORROW

Heirlooms of Tomorrow/California Originals, of Manhattan Beach and Torrance, California, was founded in 1947.

Heirlooms of Tomorrow is noted for porcelain pieces decorated with applied lace and fancy roses. In 1965, Heirlooms of Tomorrow was listed under California Originals.

1. Paper label – 1952
2. Printed
3. Current paper label

ROYAL WORCESTER

The Worcester porcelain factory was established in 1751, and in 1862 became known as Royal Worcester. The mark is a small crescent, a crown with Royal and there may or may not be a small cross. The only English porcelain factory that was established in the eighteenth century and is still in production today is that of the Worcester Royal Porcelain Company.

Royal Worcester standard mark, 1862–1875

Royal Worcester standard mark, 1876–1891; letter underneath changed every year

Royal Worcester standard mark, 1891–1963

Royal Worcester revised mark, 1959 on, used with year marks

Lenox slipper, 6¼" x 2½", decorated with pink flowers and gilding. Lenox slippers/shoes are scarce. The mark is in the gold wreath underneath. Circa 1965. $285.00.

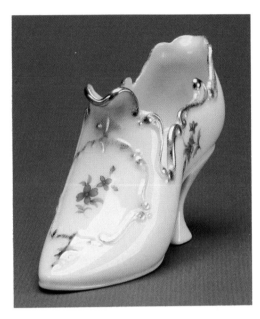

Another view of the Lenox slipper.

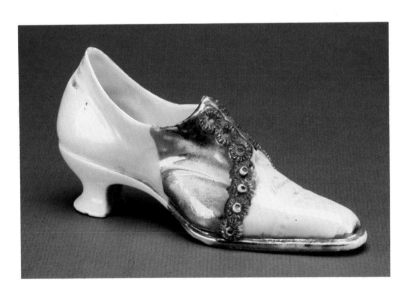

A white porcelain shoe, 6½" x 3¼", trimmed with gold flowers. Germany, circa 1900. $45.00 – 60.00.

A Bennington boot with a dog at the toe and a cat peering out of the top of the boot, 2½" x 3⅛". Circa 1900. $85.00 – 100.00.

White porcelain slipper, 5⅜" x 3¼", with an orange colored flower and green leaves hand painted on the flair. On the sole, "Victoria — Carlsbad, Austria." There is gilding on the flat bow and around the flair. Circa 1900. $120.00 – 150.00.

A pair of Meissen slippers, 2¼" x 1". $350.00 – 400.00 pr.

White Royal Bayreuth man's shoe, 5¼" x 2⅛". Circa 1920. (The Royal Bayreuth blue mark after 1891 had the word Bavaria added to it. The founding date of the factory, 1784, was incorporated into the mark, which in fact leads many people into thinking wrongly that it is the date of manufacture of the particular piece.) Royal Bayreuth has not been reproduced since 1949. These pieces are marked with a bright green. The earlier markings were blue or pale green. $200.00 – 225.00.

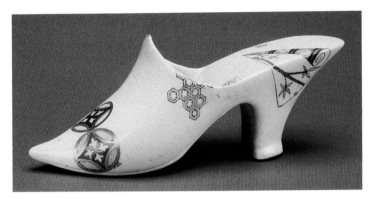

White porcelain slipper, 6" x 4½", decorated with hand-painted circles. Royal Worcester mark, circa 1876, on the sole. $250.00 – 300.00.

Orange and dark pink luster decorates this white porcelain slipper, 4½" x 2". This slipper has a flower on the vamp, circa 1900, Germany. $60.00 – 70.00.

Two white porcelain baby shoes, 4" x 3½", were produced by the Herend factory that was founded in 1839. This factory, located near Budapest, Hungary, is still producing fine porcelain today. The shoe on the **left** is decorated with hand-painted blue flowers; the shoe on the **right** with birds and flowers. Circa 1978. $45.00 – 65.00 ea.

White luster slipper, 6" x 3", is decorated with an orange stripe. Made in Czechoslovakia, circa 1920. $40.00 – 50.00.

This burnished gold porcelain slipper, 5" x 4½", is decorated with white and turquoise dots. Under the sole is the Royal Worcester mark. Circa 1883. $250.00 – 300.00.

Yellow porcelain hand-painted slipper, 6" x 4½". The Royal Worcester mark incised and stamped on the sole. Circa 1876. $250.00 – 300.00.

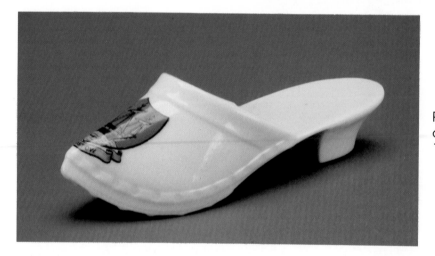

Porcelain 4¾" slipper has an emblem on the vamp with "V.H. Goss." Circa 1908. $125.00.

The sole of the above slipper has the wording "model of wooden shoes worn by the fisherwomen of Boulogne Sur Mer & Le Portal," ®^{d} #539421.

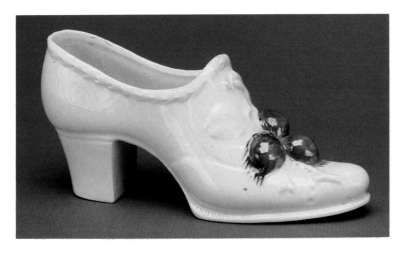

Pale green luster slipper, 4" x 2½", decorated with gilding. Circa 1920, marked "Germany." $65.00.

White porcelain shoe, 6" x 3½", decorated with lustered fruit. Circa 1900, marked "Germany." $75.00.

White porcelain slipper, 6" x 3", decorated with a gold painted flower. Circa 1906. $105.00.

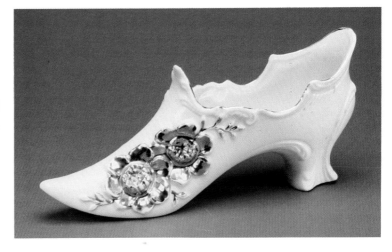

Blue bone china snakeskin court shoe, 5½cm h x 12cm l x 4½cm w, was designed by Wendy Lankester in a limited number — 200 worldwide. This hand-painted shoe from the Gainsborough collection was researched for accuracy of style. Mrs. Lankester designed two ranges; haute couture and miniature. Circa 1986. $140.00 – 160.00.

Tan pottery baby shoe, 3⅞" x 2¼", decorated with a rose, complete with leaves and openings for laces. Circa 1890. $75.00 – 85.00.

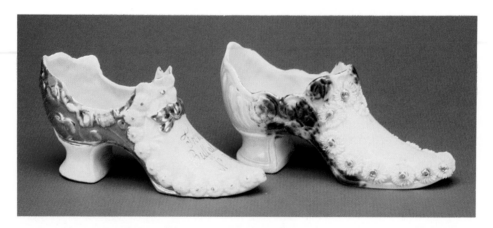

Two white porcelain slippers from Germany, both 5" x 2½". The **right** slipper is decorated with gold, the **left** with sponged blue. Both have applied rosettes. Circa 1900. $75.00 ea.

Three porcelain slippers marked "Germany." **Left** — 3¼" x 1¼" and has an applied rose and leaves. $35.00. **Middle** — 4½" x 2¼" and is decorated with an applied pink rose. $45.00. **Right** — 3¼" x 1¼", has a squatty heel and is decorated with a white applied rose. Circa 1930. $35.00.

White porcelain slipper, 4½" x 2½", is an Elfinware from Germany and is decorated with applied flowers. Circa 1900. $45.00 – 55.00.

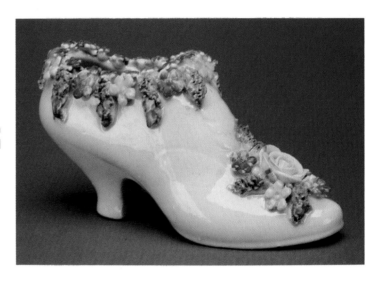

7½" porcelain shoe marked "Germany," has chickens adorning the toe and top as decoration. Circa 1910. $75.00 – 85.00.

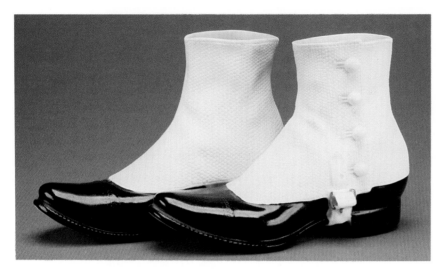

A pair of Royal Bayreuth bisque shoes, complete with spats. The quality of the shoes are indicative of Royal Bayreuth. Circa 1915 with a black mark. $700.00 – 850.00.

Pottery shoe 5", decorated with flowers on the vamp, a gilded toe, and a black heel. Marked "Czecho-slovakia." Circa 1920. $25.00.

Three hand-decorated porcelain boots. **Left** — a white boot, 4" x 2½", has a pink and bluish-green luster gilding out-lining or edging all deco-ration, near the top in gold "a present from Ireland," and under the bottom/sole "#749 – Thuringia, Germany." Circa 1910. $45.00 – 55.00. **Middle** — white boot, 3⅞" x 2½", has a dark blue, pink, and yellow luster, and a courting scene on the toe marked "Germany." Circa 1910. $40.00 –

50.00. **Right** — 4⅝" x 4⅛" white boot, decorated with muted luster sponge design and flower on front outlined with gilding. Marked "Germany" and "#1885" on the sole. Circa 1900. $40.00 – 50.00.

Gray luster, 3½" x 2" shoe, has a pink rose surrounded by blue flowers and green leaves. Marked "Germany." Circa 1935. $40.00.

A 2½" tan boot made by Frankoma Pottery Company. $35.00 – 45.00.

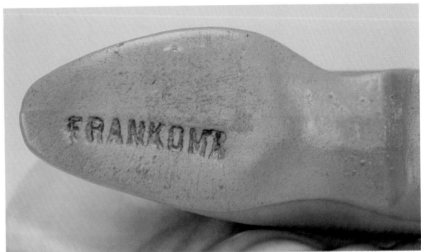

The bottom of the Frankoma boot.

A tan boot, 3" high, was made by Van Briggle Pottery Company. Circa 1930. $55.00 – 70.00.

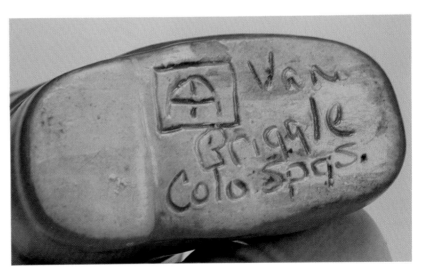

The bottom of the Van Briggle boot.

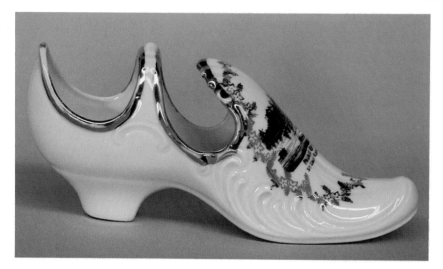

White porcelain slipper, 7" x 2¾", with a scene representing the World's Fair. Under the picture, "A Palace of Electricity. St. Louis Exposition, 1904." $185.00.

Close-up of the above slipper showing the front.

Two of the pink luster porcelain boots from Germany. **Left** — 5¾" x 2¼", decorated with a gold bird and dark blue bird. Circa 1900. $110.00. **Right** — 4⅝" x 4⅛", decorated with white flowers and dark blue leaves. Circa 1900. $55.00

White porcelain slipper, 3¾" x 2", from Germany is decorated with red berries, blue leaves, and the same texture as that of snow babies. Circa 1900. $50.00 – 65.00.

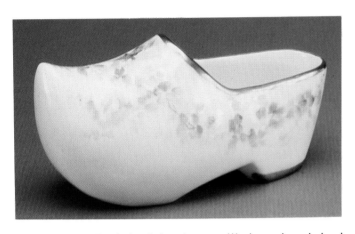

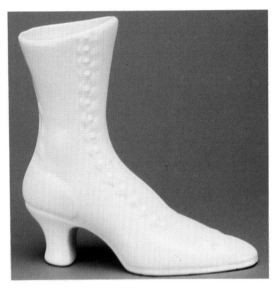

A pale blue Dutch style shoe with hand-painted flowers, 5" x 2⅛". Marked "Germany." Circa 1930. $35.00 – 50.00.

White high button shoe, 6" x 6", made by the Red Wing Pottery Company. Under the sole "Red Wing USA 651." Circa 1930. $125.00 – 150.00.

An attached pair of ceramic shoes, 3½" x 2¼", on a 3½" x ¼" base that is a match striker. Marked "Germany" on the base. Circa 1910. $65.00.

White porcelain shoe, 8¾" x 1" x 2½", with a winter scene on the vamp. Underneath "Depuis 1748-Villeroy & Boch. Ancienne Manufacture Imperiale et Royal Luxenbourgh-Naif Christmas." Circa 1978. $40.00.

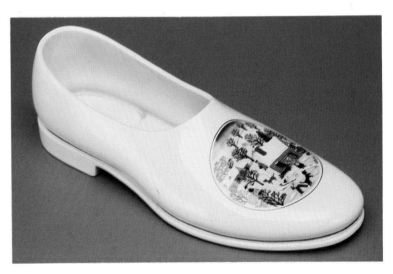

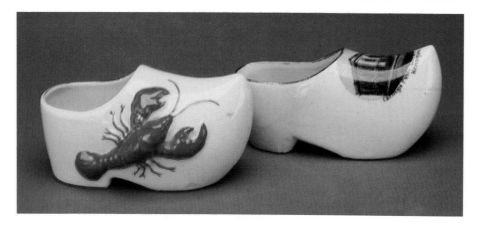

Two porcelain Dutch style shoes from Germany. **Left** — 4¼" x 2¼", has a lobster on one side, and the other side has a picture of the Royal Pavillion, Brighton. Underneath in a circle, the word "Foreign." Circa 1910. $60.00. **Right** — 4" x 2", has a picture of Carnegie Public Library and Masonic temple, Hemington, Kansas; underneath "Imported for cash market – Hemington, Kansas." Hand painted by a studio. Germany, circa 1910. $40.00.

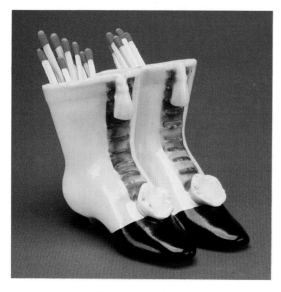

A pair of white porcelain high button shoes that hold matches. 3½" x 2", has a rough ridge on the back to strike the matches. They are decorated with a white flower, a black toe and heel, and under the bottom "Germany." Circa 1910. $75.00 – 90.00.

White porcelain shoe, 4¾" x 3¼", with a cherub on the toe. Marked "Germany." Circa 1900. $50.00 – 65.00.

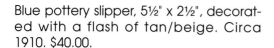

Blue pottery slipper, 5½" x 2½", decorated with a flash of tan/beige. Circa 1910. $40.00.

28

Two porcelain German-made shoes. **Left** — white, 4⅞" x 3", with a buckle and crest. "3587-Germany" on the sole. Circa 1920. $45.00 – 55.00. **Right** — a white porcelain shoe, 5" x 2¼", shaded with pink and gilding as decoration. "Jersey City, N.J." on the side, "Germany" on the back of the heel. Circa 1920. $60.00 – 70.00.

A white porcelain shoe, 2½" x 2", with pastel flowers made by Royal Adderley of England. Circa 1978. $25.00.

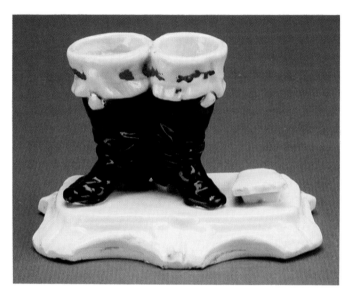

A pair of porcelain boots 3" high for matches on a 1" x 4" base with a striker on the right side of the boots. Marked "Germany." Circa 1910. $60.00 – 75.00.

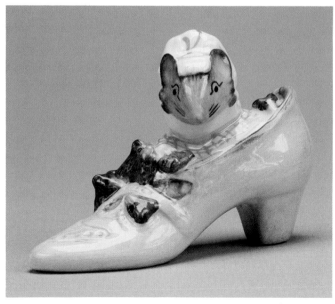

A blue Beatrix Potter's "The old woman who lived in a shoe," 3½" x 1¾". Royal Doulton mark. Circa 1959. $30.00.

White porcelain Dutch style slipper, 3½" x 1¼", hand painted with flowers, decorated with gilding. Marked "Limoges." Circa 1968. $30.00 – 40.00.

The high men's shoe, 2¾" x 4", has laces and clear stitching designs on the toe and side of the shoe. Marked Royal Bayreuth. Circa 1920. $175.00 – 250.00.

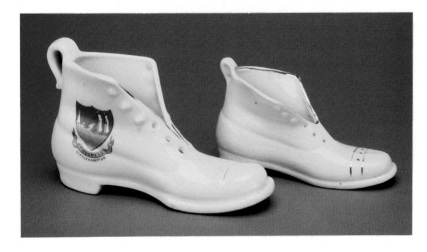

Two white porcelain men's shoes. **Left** — 5¼" x 3" has a crest on the side with the wording "Progress-Little Hampton CZECHOSLOVAKIA" on the sole. $45.00 – 55.00. **Right** — 3¼" x 2", does not have any decoration. Marked "Germany." Circa 1920. $45.00 – 55.00.

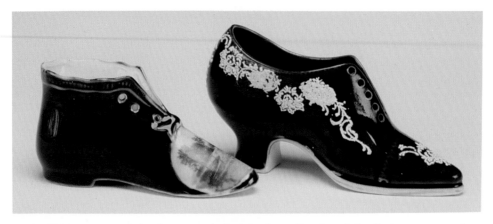

Cobalt blue porcelain shoe and slipper from England, both have openings for laces and open to the toe. **Left** — baby shoe, 3½" x 2", has a hand-painted scene across the vamp. Circa 1920. $50.00 – 65.00. **Right** — 4½" x 3", has white painted flowers across the back and sides. Circa 1900. $75.00 – 90.00.

White luster shoe, 3¼" x 1⅝", with a cat on the vamp of the shoe. Circa 1952. "Souvenir from Canada" on the maple leaf. Marked "Germany." $25.00 – 30.00.

Gray luster shoe, 4¾" x 2¼", with white flowers on the front of the shoe and openings for laces and marked "Germany." Circa 1920. $35.00 – 50.00.

Black matte Gouda slipper, 4¼" x 1¾", stylized in the Art Nouveau design, circa 1930. Under the bottom (on the sole) "Regina-Gouda-Holland-I-Sontella X." $150.00 – 175.00.

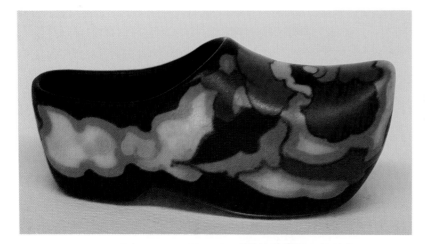

Black matte Gouda slipper, 4¾" x 2¼", Art Nouveau style. Circa 1930, marked "Regina-Gouda-Holland." $150.00 – 175.00.

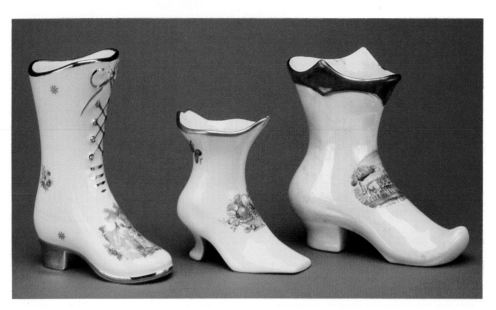

Three Limoges boot/high shoes. **Left** — a white porcelain boot, 4" x 3", with a courting scene on the toe, decorated with gilding. Circa 1950. $45.00. **Middle** — a high shoe, decorated with a basket of fruit and gilding, 3½" x 3¼". Circa 1950. $35.00. **Right** — a white luster boot, 3¾" x 3", with a "transfer" scene, decorated with gilding and burgundy-colored trim. Circa 1950. $25.00.

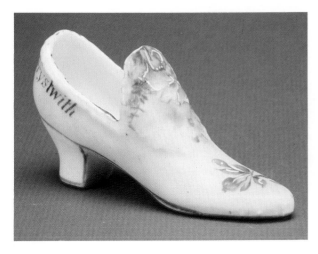

A white satin Austrian porcelain slipper, 3⅝" x 1¾", decorated with hand-painted flowers on the toe and vamp. Across the back of the heel, "a present from Aberystwith" under the sole, "Made in Austria." Circa 1920. $125.00.

A burgundy ceramic mule, 5½" x 2", with a flash of yellow across the vamp. Marked "Made in Belgium." Circa 1936. $60.00.

Burgundy glossy slipper, 4" x 1¾", decorated with gold circles. Under the sole, "Goudewaagen-Gouda-Holland." Circa 1930. $100.00.

Blue and white hand-painted box in the shoe shape, 5" x 3". Marked "Limoges." Circa 1990. $125.00 – 150.00.

Another view of the shoe-shaped box by Limoge.

Pale grayish-blue luster slipper, 4" x 2½", decorated with a pink rose and green leaves. Circa 1920 and marked "Germany." $50.00.

White porcelain boot, 4½" x 3¾", decorated with flowers and butterflies, two pink bows on the buttons, gilding on the scalloped top. "Germany" on the bottom. $35.00.

White porcelain high shoe, 3¼" x 2¼", with a crest or emblem "Hawkhurst." Marked "England." Circa 1920. $50.00.

A pink luster slipper, 5¼" x 2¾", on one half a gold flower. This slipper was commonly referred to as a cabinet piece where the most decorated side would be shown. Photograph was taken on the gold side. Circa 1900, marked "Germany." $50.00 – 65.00.

White ceramic slipper, 4¾" x 2¾", with hand-painted flowers on the toe and both sides. Marked "James Kent-old Foley-made in England." Circa 1980. $40.00.

Two German porcelain slippers. **Left** — pink slipper, 4¼" x 1¾", with a little black shoe string. The heel and around the sole decorated in black. Circa 1900. $45.00. **Right** — pale pink low-cut slipper, 4¼" x 1¾" x 2¼" at highest, the front trimmed in white. Circa 1890. $45.00.

Left — cobalt blue slipper, 5" x 2¼", with white applied flowers trimmed with flecks of gold. Circa 1900, Germany. $60.00. **Right** — a cobalt blue with white toe bow slipper, hand painted in pale orange flowers and blue leaves outlined in gold. Circa 1900, unmarked. $50.00.

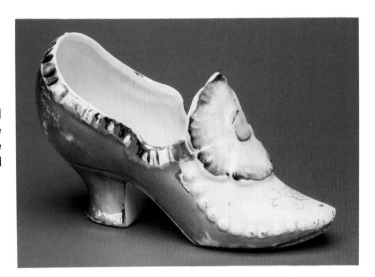

Large white porcelain slipper, 6¼" x 3½", painted gold over most of the slipper except for the front, where a large purple pansy adorns the top of the opening. Circa 1915, unmarked (the style appears to be German). $50.00.

Three Elfinware (Germany) slippers, each decorated and trimmed with a mass of flowers and a mass of greenery. **Left** — flat slipper, 3¾" x 1½". **Middle** — 4¼" x 2¼". **Right** — slipper with the same flowers, greenery, and the squatty heel is trimmed in green. Circa 1920. (Elfinware was made in Germany from about 1920 until 1940. The slippers are characterized by the tiny applied flowers that often cover the entire surface.) $65.00 ea.

White ceramic slipper, 4⅛" x 2¼", decorated in brown, blue, and green stripes. Circa +1890. (An antique store in Columbus, Ohio, provided a statement in writing that this was one of the few American-made slippers during the 1900s when the focus was utilitarian.) Produced in the Pennsylvania area. $65.00.

Chalkware red plaid slipper, 4" x 1¼", with a little black Scottie on the toe. Circa 1915. Marked "Manor Ware," on the side R^d 873013. $65.00.

Four pairs of porcelain slippers. **First** — white, 2¼" x 1¼", with a pink flower, green leaves across the front, and blue trim around the top opening. Circa 1930, marked "Made in Japan." $25.00. **Second** — white, with blue applied flowers , 2½" x 1¼". Circa 1930, marked "Germany." $30.00. **Third** — white, 2¼" x 1¼", with a white flower between the pair. Circa 1930, marked "Japan." $25.00. **Fourth** — white, 2½" x 1¼", with a white rose and green leaves between the pair. Circa 1930, marked "Germany." $25.00 – 35.00 ea.

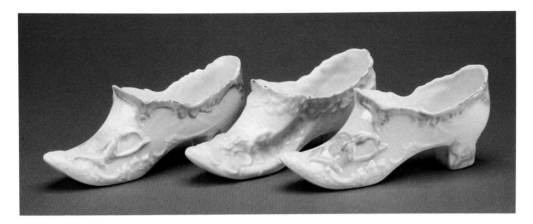

Three white 4¾" x 2" porcelain cabinet slippers, circa 1900. Marked "Germany."
Left — decorated with pink flowers on the right side of the slipper, including the right side of the heel. **Middle** — decorated with blue flower and vine on the right side of the slipper. **Right** — the same as the blue except the entire slipper is tan (beige), with the right side decorated with pale green flower and vine. $45.00 ea.

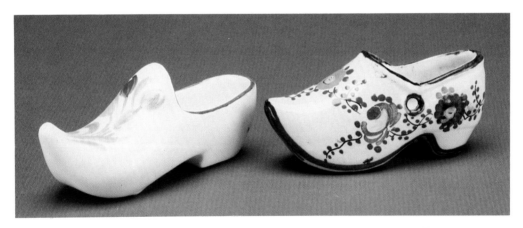

Left — white slipper, 4" x 1½", hand-painted with pastel flowers, green leaves, and blue around the opening. Circa 1950, marked "Best Bone Denton China – England." $35.00. **Right** — white ceramic slipper, 3½" x 1¾, with hand-painted flowers and leaves. Circa 1960, marked "Made in France." The paper label from Bloomingdale's , New York, is still under the bottom. $50.00.

Left — blue ceramic shoe, 4" x 2¼", with a cat perched between the buttons. Circa 1900, Germany. $50.00. **Right** — blue slipper, 3" x 1⅛", with flowers decorating the entire shoe. Circa 1960, marked "Brazil." $25.00.

Left — a red Santa boot, 2⅝" x 3¼", trimmed in black. Circa 1969. Marked "Goebel, West Germany." $35.00. **Right** — blue slipper, 4½" x 2¾", decorated with flowers on the toe. Circa 1980. Marked "Portugal." $25.00.

Three hand-painted Delft blue Dutch shoes. **Left** — 6¼" x 2¾". $25.00. **Middle** — 3½" x 1¾". $15.00. **Right** — a pair, 2¼" x ¾". $15.00. They are all decorated with the popular Holland windmills. Circa 1960.

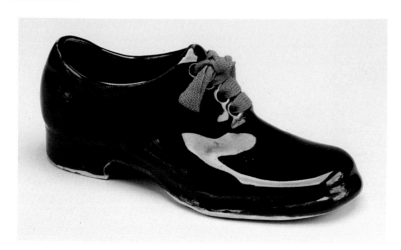

A brown Bennington men's shoe, 6" x 2¼", with laces. Circa 1920. $65.00 – 75.00.

Four small porcelain shoes/slippers from Germany. **First** — pale pink, 2¼" x 1¾" shoe with a Cuban heel, decorated with a white rose and three tiny blue flowers. Circa 1930. $40.00. **Second** — pale gray luster shoe, 2¾" x 1¾", with tiny blue flowers from the toe to the top. Circa 1950. $30.00. **Third** — pale pink shoe, 2¾" x 1¾",

with a white rose and tiny blue flowers. Circa 1950. $30.00. **Fourth** — white slipper, 3" x ¾", with a rose on the toe. Circa 1920. $40.00.

Green oxford, 4¾" x 2⅛", with six openings for laces. Circa 1950. $40.00.

A boot, 5½" x 6¾", with a decal on the front of a building in Germany. The boot is decorated with stylized flowers and vines. Circa 1950, marked "Germany." $35.00 – 45.00.

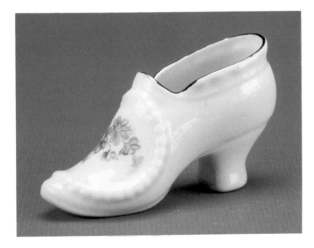

White porcelain slipper, 3¼" x 2", with pastel flowers across the front. Circa 1950, marked "Made in England." $25.00 – 35.00.

Blue and white brogan, 5¼" x 3¾", with a colonial scene and openings for laces. Circa 1960. Marked "Old Foley – James Kent Staffordshire, England." $35.00 – 45.00.

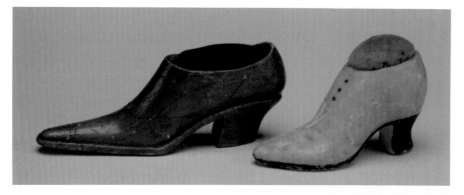

Left — a wooden shoe pin cushion, 7" x 3¼", carved and detailed. $40.00. **Right** — a pale green porcelain pin cushion, 5" x 3¾", with a pink cushion. Circa 1900, unmarked. $45.00.

Left — a white porcelain slipper, 3¼" x 2", with a decal bust of George Washington. Circa 1939. $25.00. **Middle** — white shoe, 3¾" x 1¼", with a painted buckle and a bust of George Washington on the toe. Marked "Mt. Vernon, Virginia." $35.00. **Right** — the same shoe with Martha Washington on the toe. $25.00.

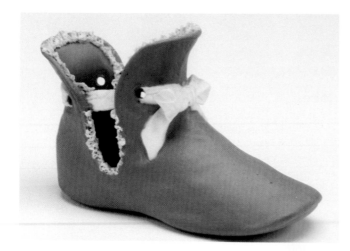

Green 4½" x 2¼" open-sided ceramic slipper, trimmed with a white bow. $30.00.

Yellow ceramic shoe, 6" x 2½", trimmed with flowers. Circa 1950, marked "Germany." $45.00.

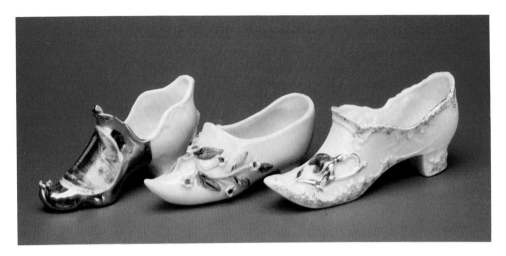

Left — white porcelain slipper, 4⅜" x 2¼", with a decal on the front of the shoe of 14th and Fapnam Streets, Omaha, Nebraska. Circa 1910, marked "Germany." $30.00. **Middle** — white porcelain cabinet shoe, 4¾" x 2", decorated with gold on the right side. Circa 1900, marked "Germany." $30.00 – 40.00. **Right** — ceramic slipper, 4" x 1¾", decorated with blue applied flowers, green vines, and leaves. Circa 1900, marked "Germany." $45.00 – 55.00.

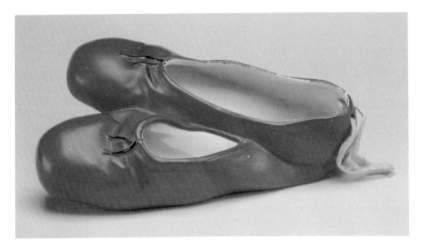

Red ballerina shoes 9" long. Circa 1950, marked "Germany." $25.00 – 35.00.

Left — a tan brogan, 2" x 1½", with tiny flowers. Circa 1970, marked "Italy." $15.00. **Right** — a pair of white pottery mules, 2½" x 1¼", painted flowers and the word "Strausbourg" on the side. Circa 1900. $50.00.

Green ceramic humidor, 6" x 8½", with two indentations for pipes. Circa 1920, marked "Made in England." $65.00 – 75.00.

A pair of ceramic men's shoes, 4" x 3", with laces and fine details. Circa 1930. $55.00.

Left — white porcelain shoe, 3¼" x 1¾", with a crest on the front. Circa 1930, marked "Germany." $35.00. **Middle** — white porcelain brogan, 3" x 2¼", with roses decorating the shoe and gold laces. Circa 1970, marked "Fine bone china – made in England." $25.00. **Right** — white porcelain Dutch style, 3¼" x 1¾", decorated with a rose on the toe. Circa 1960. Marked "Fine bone china – Sanford – Made in England." $25.00.

Blue ceramic hand-painted shoe marked "China," 3¾" x 1½". This style is representative of the time when young Chinese girls from wealthy families had wrapped feet. $75.00 – 90.00.

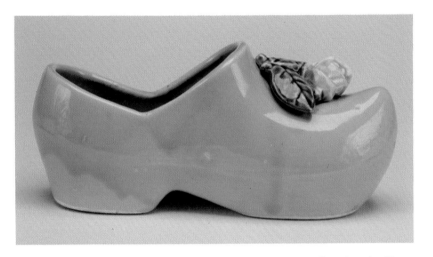

Turquoise slipper, 7" x 3½" with a pink flower on the front. Circa 1950, marked "McCoy." $45.00.

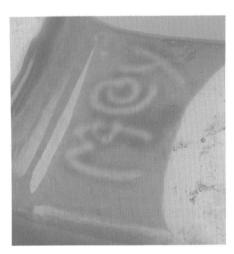

The sole of the previous slipper to show the mark.

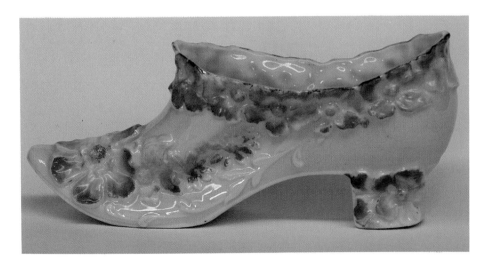

White cabinet shoe, 7" x 2¾", decorated with pastel lavender flowers around the top and on the side and heel. Marked "Germany." Circa 1906. $55.00 – 65.00.

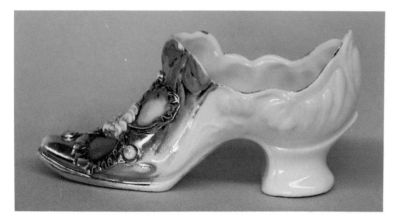

White porcelain slipper, 4½" x 2", has muted luster flowers in blue and pink, a white center, and gilding covering the rest of the front of the shoe. Marked "Germany." Circa 1899. $65.00 – 80.00.

Brown shoe, 3½" x 1¾", with holes for laces. This shoe was bought in Greece in 1976, date unknown. $45.00.

Turquoise pottery slipper, 7" x 2¼", with a square toe and four buttons on both sides. The shoe was described by the dealer as a Pilgrim shoe. $35.00.

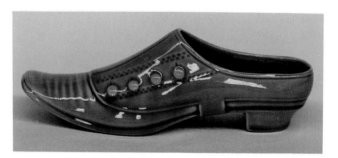

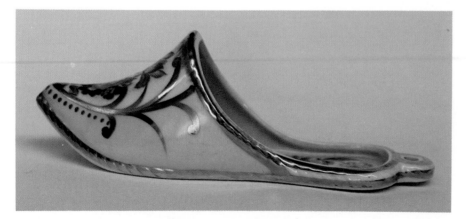

Yellow porcelain hand-painted hanging slipper, 5½" x 2¼", has gilding around the entire slipper. The flowers decorate the toe and inside. Circa 1920. $50.00 – 65.00.

Right — Another view of the same slipper.

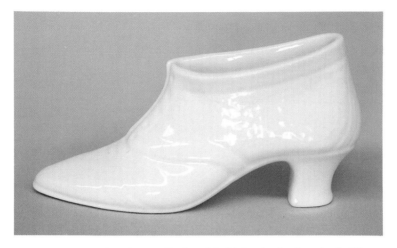

White porcelain shoe, 5½" x 3", "Made in Spain." Circa 1960. $25.00.

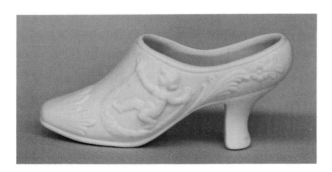

White bisque slipper, 2" x ¾", decorated with flowers by relief. Circa 1950. $20.00.

An old established pattern, country roses on a white English porcelain slipper, 4⅛" x 3". Circa 1950. $30.00.

A white German porcelain boot, 3⅛" x 5", decorated with pink flowers and gilding. Circa 1950. $30.00.

A pair of Korean porcelain slippers, 2½" x ¾". Circa 1980. $10.00 – 12.00 pair.

A German porcelain slipper, 4¾" x 2", decorated with gold on the entire front. On the front, "A present from Edinbourough." Circa 1920. $70.00.

Blue and white large porcelain boot, 11½" high x 9" long. From England, circa 1920. $200.00.

A pearlized, flower-decorated porcelain slipper, 4¾" x 2⅛", the roses and leaves decorate the front. Circa 1936. $15.00 – 20.00.

Three blue and white high shoes, hand decorated, slight variations in each boot. Paper label "Made in Taiwan." $5.00– 8.00.

A pottery boot, 3¾" high x 3" with blue decoration. Paper label "Made in Taiwan." Circa 1989. $5.00 – 8.00.

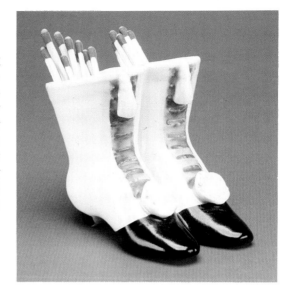

A pair of white ceramic high shoes decorated with black across the toe, a pom-pon on the toe, and a tassel hanging from the top. The striker is attached to the back of the boot, circa 1890. $75.00. Before the invention of the safety match in 1855, matches were carefully handled and kept in match boxes because they ignited easily. During the early 1800s, matches were considered a necessity in every household and were used for lighting candles, wood, or coal. Match holders in shoe shapes were common and found in many homes. Today these match holders are collectible — one collector has over 800 match holders.

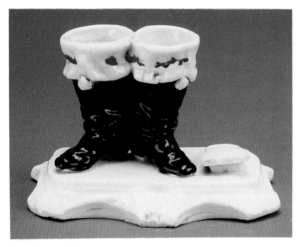

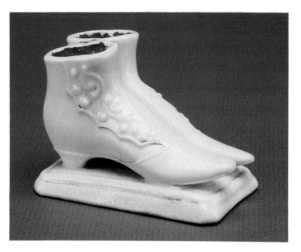

A pair of porcelain boots painted black with a white fur trim on a base. The striker is on the side next to the boots, circa 1890. $95.00.

White ceramic shoes on a base. The shoes are buttoned. The base has the striker on the side. Circa 1890. $90.00.

Pink luster boot, 4¾" x 4¼" h, applied decoration with two gold birds. Circa 1918. Marked "Germany." $70.00.

Pink luster shoe, 5¾" x 3" h, with open eyelets, applied ringlets. On the toe is written "Souvenir of Uniontown Pa." Circa 1920, marked "Germany". $85.00.

Pale blue shoe held by an elf. A flower adorns the toe. The shoe measures 3½" x 1¼". Marked "Austria." $75.00.

Royal Bayreuth ladies' high shoe, 4⅜" x 4" h, open eyelets and fine details. Circa 1930. $200.00.

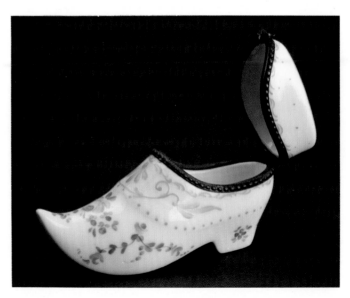

A Limoges shoe, 3¼" x 1¾", with hinged lid making this a shoe box; decorated with hand-painted flowers. Circa 1980. $130.00.

The open shoe-shaped box.

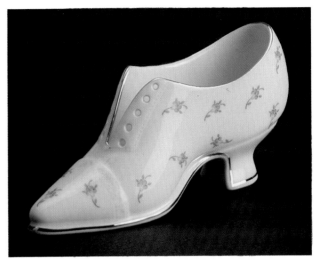

A variegated shoe in blue, green, and tan marked "Made in Holland." Circa 1960. $45.00.

White shoe, 5½" x 2¾", with tiny blue flowers hand painted over entire shoe. The open eyelets could accommodate shoe strings. Marked "Tettau – Germany ANNO 1890." $100.00.

A large porcelain shoe, 7" x 4¼", with slightly turned toe, decorated with a gold bow and gold outlining the design on the shoe. Marked "Heirlooms of Tomorrow – Made in USA." Circa 1954. $100.00.

A pair of baby shoes marked "47C-L & 47C–R Metlox – Made in USA." Circa 1941. The Metlox Potteries of Manhattan Beach, California, was in business from 1927 to 1985. $80.00 pair.

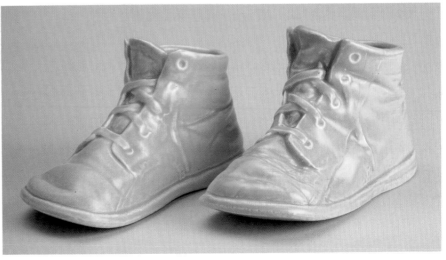

A pair of white porcelain boots with traces of gold. The base has a striker on the right. Circa 1890. $75.00.

A pair of white porcelain boots with traces of gold and red, the same as the top left photo except for the striker on the left. Circa 1890. $75.00.

A pair of pale blue shoes with five buttons on the right and left shoe. The base has the striker on the side. Circa 1890. $75.00.

A white porcelain shoe, 6¾" x 3½", with a large white raised flower and leaves across the front extending to the back. There are six open eyelets near the V opening and gold paint at the top front. Germany, circa 1918. $100.00. A note in the shoe states "Dresden slipper found in old barn in Kansas in 1930 or about that date, origin unknown."

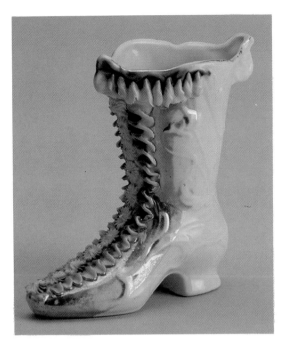

White porcelain boot, 3¾" x 4¼" decorated with applied blue ribbon-type porcelain and white daisies in the center from the top to the toe. $65.00.

A white porcelain baby bootee, 4" x 2", with six open eyelets and a small embossed bow. Tiny pink flower decals are around the top and over the entire shoe. Austria, circa 1930. $75.00.

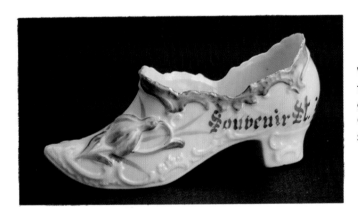

White porcelain cabinet shoe with pink flowers on one side and trimmed with green on the show. "Souvenir — St. Louis." Circa 1930. "Made in Germany" on the sole. $50.00 – 65.00.

White porcelain shoe with strap across the instep. An applied flower decorated with gold and white applied leaves. Germany, circa 1918. $70.00 – 85.00.

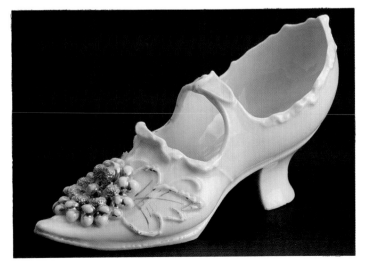

A Faience blue pottery shoe, 3½" x 1¼," decorated with stylized flowers and scrolls. Marked with the artist's initials or company. France, circa 1920. $100.00.

A pottery shoe, 7" x 1¾", decorated with pink and maroon flowers. Marked "Regina 432 WB Delft Road, Made in Holland." Circa 1940. $65.00.

A white porcelain shoe, 5¾" x 2½", with a lad in yellow pants sitting on the toe and fox near the heel. The toe is trimmed in green. Circa 1920. Marked "Germany." $65.00.

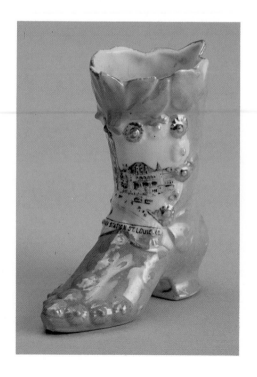

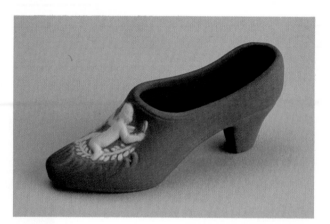

A wedgewood blue shoe, 2¼" x 1¼", with a white cherub on the toe. Marked "5149 B. Germany." $65.00.

Left: A pink luster boot, 3¼" x 3¾", with a scene of Union Station. "St. Louis, Mo" on the front. Circa 1920, Germany. $70.00 – 80.00.

Three pairs and 14 single slippers

Back row, (**left** to **right**): Red pair; 1½" x ¾"; marked "Japan." $20.00 pair. Blue Dutch style; 1½" x ¾"; marked "China." $15.00. Burgundy Dutch style; 1¼" x ¾"; with gold decoration near the toe; marked "Limoges – France." $20.00. Blue high heel; 1½" x ¾"; with a pink decal flower in front; marked "Japan." $25.00. Blue high heel; 1¼" x 1"; trimmed with gold; marked "Limoges." $20.00. Orange high heel; 1" x ¾"; with a small bow and around the top trimmed with gold; marked "Germany." $20.00. Black slipper same as sixth. $20.00. Gold 1¼" x ¾" high heel; marked "Japan." $25.00. Blue Dutch style; 1¼" x ¾"; same as third. $10.00. Front row, (**left** to **right**): Blue bisque 2" x¼" pair attached by a bird; marked "Japan." $35.00. Blue flat mule; 1¾" x ⅛"; trimmed in gold; marked "Limoges – France." $20.00. Black high heel trimmed in gold; marked "Japan." $25.00. Gold 1¼" x ¾" high heel; marked "Japan." $25.00. Gold high heel; 1¾" x ¾"; marked "Japan." $20.00. Blue high heel; 1" x ¾"; with a pink applied flower and green leaves; marked "Germany." $25.00. Teal blue high heel; 1" x ¾"; trimmed in gold; marked "Germany." $20.00. A pair of gold 1½" x ¾" slippers; marked "Japan." $20.00.

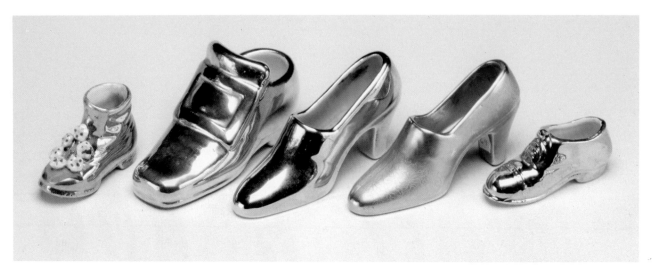

Gold slippers and shoes

Left to **right**: 1" x ¾"; decorated with white flowers; marked "Japan." $18.00. 4¼" x 2"; has a large buckle; marked "Japan." $15.00. 4" x 2¼"; plain; marked "Dixon Art Studio." $25.00. 4" x 2¼" with an embossed design; unmarked. $20.00. Man's shoe; 3" x 1¼"; laced and tied; marked "Japan." $15.00.

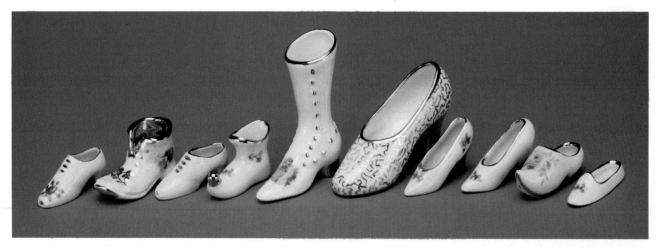

Limoges slippers/shoes

Left to **right**: 1¾" x ½" white porcelain with a pink flower on the toe. $15.00. A white porcelain brogan; 1¾" x 1"; with a gold rose on the toe and near the back; inside of the shoe is gold. $20.00. White porcelain; 1¾" x ½"; trimmed with gold. $15.00. White porcelain jester-type shoe; 1¾" x 1". $20.00. White porcelain high shoe; 3⅞" x 2¼"; decorated with gold buttons and a courting scene on the toe. $25.00. White porcelain high heel; 3½" x 1¾"; with designs in gold over the entire shoe, except the heel which is gold. $25.00. White high heel; 2" x 1"; with three flowers — one on the toe and on both sides. $20.00. White porcelain 2" x 1" high heel with a single flower near the toe. $25.00. Dutch style; 2" x ½"; has a pink flower near the vamp. $15.00.

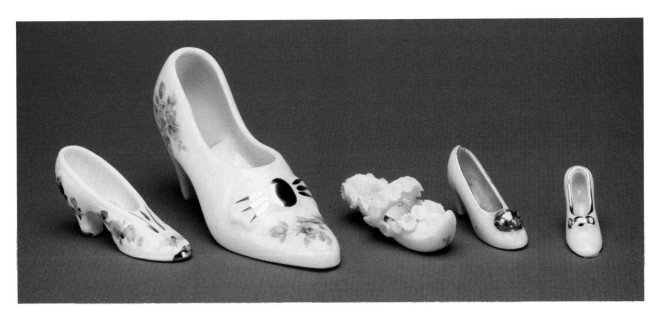

Left to **right**: White porcelain, 2½" x 1¼", painted with yellow, blue, red, and pink flowers; a butterfly on the toe and inside of the slipper; marked "Fine Bone China," "Made in England." $18.00. White porcelain high heel, 4½" x 2", with painted flowers; marked "Limoges." $25.00. White porcelain, 2⅛" x ¾", decorated with white applied flowers; marked "Germany." $20.00. White porcelain, 2" x 1¼", high heel with a gold ball on the toe; marked "Limoges – France." $20.00. White porcelain, 1" x ¾", trimmed with a gold bow; marked "Germany." $25.00.

Left to **right**: Blue Dutch style, 3¼" x 1", decorated with a courting scene in gold; marked "Limoges – France." $20.00. Gold high heel, 2¼" x 1¾"; marked "Japan." $20.00. Gold, 2½" x 1¾", with a strap and bow; marked "Japan." $20.00. Blue bisque, 2½" x 1⅛", decorated with pink flowers; "Souvenir of Long Beach Calif" on one side; marked "Japan." $25.00. Gold, 2¾" x 1¾", with a bow near the toe; marked "Japan." $20.00. Same as the fifth. $25.00. Blue 2" x 2¼" high boot, decorated with a courting scene in gold on the top and heel; marked "Limoges – France." $20.00. Gold high shoe, 2" x 1¾", laced; marked "Japan." $20.00. Gold shoe, 1¼" x 1¼", with a bow; marked "Japan." $20.00. High black shoe, 1¾" x 1¾", decorated with silver around the top; marked "Japan." $15.00.

STUDIO POTTERY

Studio pottery is made in almost every major city and many towns. This pottery is largely individual hand-made wares, normally pottery rather than porcelain. The potter has personal control from start to finish. This is in contrast to a factory where the design is conceived by one or more people, passed on to others to make the slipper or item, and then to the decorators, and finally to others for firing. The studio potter is normally responsible for all of this and, as a result, these slippers display their personal taste and ability.

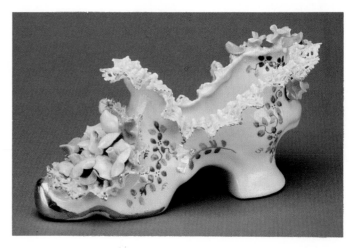

Pottery slipper with applied flowers, 4½" x 3", has lace around the top, styled as an old-fashioned slipper. Circa 1950. $25.00.

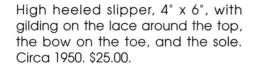

Pale beige shoe, 4½" x 3", has an applied red flower with vines and leaves. Circa 1940. $20.00.

High heeled slipper, 4" x 6", with gilding on the lace around the top, the bow on the toe, and the sole. Circa 1950. $25.00.

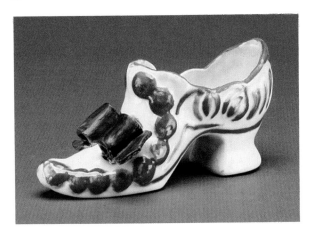

Blue and white slipper, 4⅞" x 2¼", with bow inserted through the opening across the vamp. Circa 1950. $25.00.

The Chinese slipper, 3" x 2", pale blue with the Daisy and Button design. Circa 1950. $15.00.

White porcelain slipper, 4" x 2", trimmed with lace and decorated with pastel flowers and gilding. Marked "Heirlooms of Tomorrow." Circa 1950. $25.00. (Heirlooms of Tomorrow/ California Originals, Manhattan Beach and Torrance, California. Heirlooms of Tomorrow was listed for porcelain figurines, shoes, slippers, and other miniatures from 1948 to 1953. The name was changed officially to California Originals.) $30.00 – 35.00.

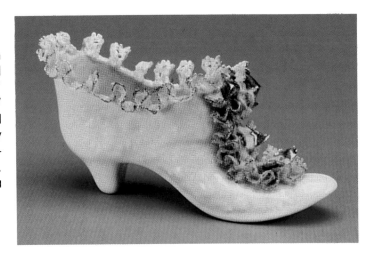

High heeled slipper, 5" x 3¼", painted by Constance Martinella. Circa 1962. Marked " Made in Brazil." $35.00.

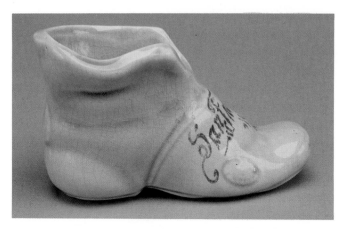

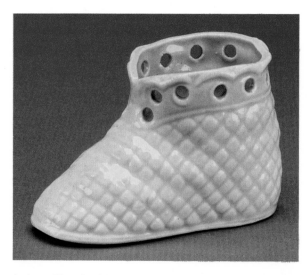

Blue heavy pottery slipper, 3" x 3", with "San Francisco. 1936" across the vamp. $35.00.

A tan 3" x 2⅛" bootee with holes around the top and four holes for laces in the front. $25.00.

Blue high heeled shoe, 4¼" x 5⅛", is hand painted by Eva Savage. $30.00.

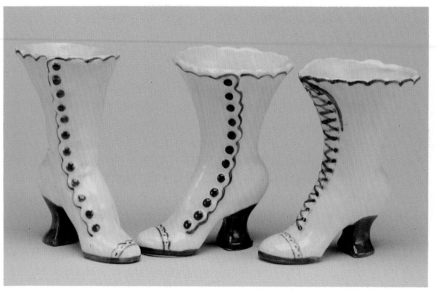

"Laguna Pottery Studio" high shoes, 3½" x 4½". **Left** is trimmed in turquoise on the buttons down the right side, across the toe, the scalloping around the top, heel, and sole. **Middle** is same as the **left**, except for the brown color. **Right** is a slightly different style trimmed in turquoise with laced strings. $40.00 ea.

Turquoise slipper, 4¼" x 2", with a pink rose as decoration. $20.00.

Turquoise slipper, 3½" x 2½", has an applied flower on the vamp as decoration. Circa 1930. $25.00.

White heavy slipper, 4½" x 2⅛", with applied pastel flowers on each side and the front. $18.00.

Iridescent high-heeled slipper, 4" x 2½". $20.00 – 25.00.

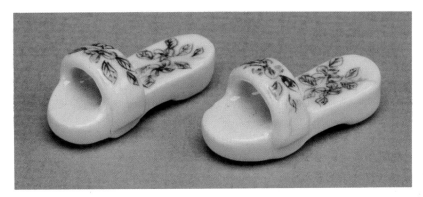

A pair of one-inch sandals, hand painted with flowers. $20.00 pair.

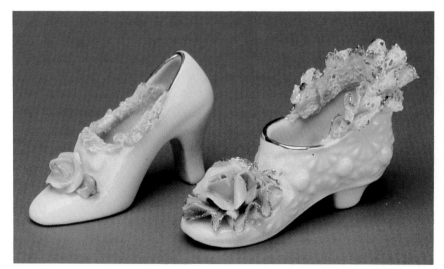

Two Heirlooms of Tomorrow shoes. **Left**: white 2" x 1¼" slipper with a yellow rose. **Right**: white slipper with a pink rose. Both have lace as decoration and a trademark of Heirlooms of Tomorrow Pottery Co. $35.00 each.

Three hand-painted and decorated slippers, each trimmed with gold in addition to the pink flowers. **Left**: 3" x 2¼". $18.00. **Middle**: 2" x 2⅛". $18.00. **Right**: 2" x 2". $18.00.

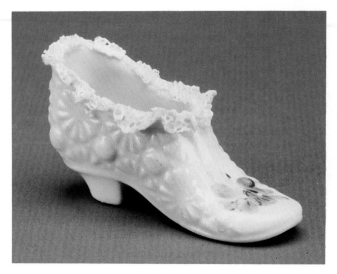

White 2" x 1¼" ceramic slipper with Daisy and Button pattern, decal near the toe, and lace around the top. Another Heirloom of Tomorrow. $35.00.

Gray slipper, 4" x 2½", trimmed with a gold flower. Marked "USA." $20.00.

Gold ceramic slipper, 4¼" x 1¾", has a pale blue lining and is marked "Dixon Art Studio." 22 karat gold. $35.00.

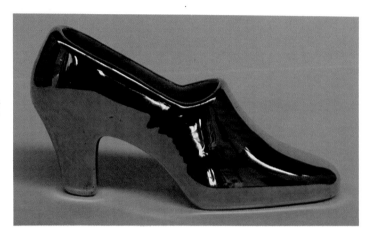

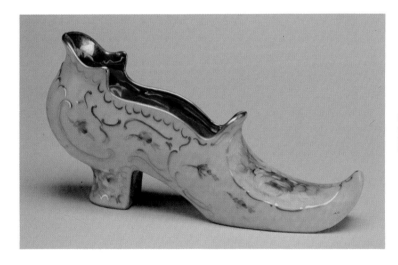

A large porcelain slipper, 7" x 4½", hand-painted pink flowers on a pale green background. Circa 1965. $20.00.

A white porcelain shoe, 6" x 2¼", decorated with decals and blue heel and toe. $25.00.

Left — green porcelain slipper, 4⅜" x 1⅜", with traces of blue. **Middle** — dark green high shoe, 5¼" x 4½". **Right** — brown slipper, 4⅜" x 1⅜", with a flash of red. All of these shoes have a paper label – "McMaster Craft, Dundas, Canada." $10.00 – 12.00 ea.

A ceramic large shoe, 5" x 8", with a cherub on the toe and lace around the entire top of the shoe. Marked "Heirlooms of Tomorrow." $65.00 – 75.00.

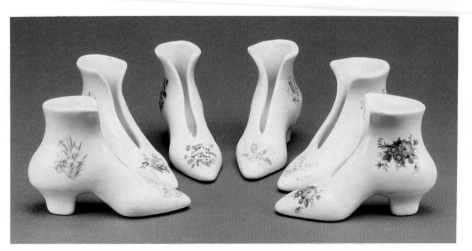

Six place card holders, 2½" x 2". Each one has a different flower as decoration. $50.00 set of six.

GLASS SLIPPERS AND SHOES

PRODUCTION

Some collectors of glass slippers, shoes, and boots obtain pleasure from collecting without any knowledge of how shoes were made. Yet there are those with a slight acquaintance to the overall process who view the knowledge as an enhancement to collecting. Glassmaking is generally considered to be America's first industry. If a glass shoe is pressed, immediately we know that it is purely a nineteenth century innovation. American glass houses produced more pressed glass slippers than England's manufacturers.

Glass is so commonplace that it is easy to forget what a remarkable and versatile substance it is. It is an artificial product that is formed by fusing together mixtures of the silica in the form of sand, potash, soda, lime, magnesia, aluminum, and lead in various proportions. "It is not known how glass first came to be made, but many unfounded accounts survive," according to Emma Paper in her book *The Illustrated Guide to American Glass,* which clearly discusses the study of glass. Glass chemistry offers an interesting sideline to the glass collector with scientific learnings or even plain curiosity about what combination of elements have gone into the making of a glass slipper. Glass has been made from an infinite number of possible glassmaking combinations, all of which were discovered painstakingly and only after centuries of trial and error experimentation by generations of glassmen. Their use of metallic oxides is responsible for the colors found in glass. These colors are derived by grinding minerals or mineral earths to powder, or by making special preparations form gold, silver, copper, or iron.

Most silica contains impurities that give glass a natural green, brown, or aquamarine color. The clear or colorless glass slipper/shoes require a pure sand and the addition of manganese as decolorizer. Instead of acting as a decolorizing agent, manganese, when added in greater amounts, will produce light purple or dark purple to black. Blues of various shades are achieved by adding cobalt or copper oxide; yellow-greens are formed with uranium oxide. Red can be made by the addition of gold, copper, or today, the less expensive chemical, selenium. Pink glass is created by using less copper or gold. This color is not often encountered in glass made before the nineteenth century.

There may be collectors who want to know whether their glass slipper was made of soda-lime or whether it has flux of potash which shows a greenish tinge. If the shoe has lead or flint, it will have a crystal clarity. It takes a skilled eye to detect the differences between lead glass and highly refined soda-lime variety. The differences can be seen by anyone who uses an ultraviolet light; lead glass will fluoresce in tints of blue, soda glass in tints of yellow. To be a able to recognize types of glass enhances one's ability to purchase slippers wisely.

McClinton, in her book, *Popular Antiques,* commented that all types of glass are made into shoe and slipper forms, including blown glass, case glass, engraved glass, spatter glass, black opaque glass, pressed glass, cut, and threaded glass.

According to Lee in her book, *Victorian Glass,* some of the oldest types of glass footwear are the blown bottles in the shape of boots made in a swirl pattern in crystal and sapphire blue. These boots of Nailsea type have no markings except the pontil mark on the bottom.

The largest selection of antique glass slippers were pressed rather than blown in many patterns.

COMMON OR NATURAL GLASS COLORS

Amber

Aquamarine

Olive, amber

Olive, green

} From the natural presence of ferrous iron (green) or ferric iron (yellow) in the sand

ARTIFICIAL COLORS

Light blue	cupric (copper) oxide
Deep sapphire blue	cobalt oxide
Brilliant red	gold chloride
Ruby red	cuprous oxide, called hammer scale

} each produces a colorless glass which turns deep red after reheating

Amethyst, purple	manganese silicate (pyrolusite) in small quantity
Brown or deep yellow	manganese silicate in larger quantity
Orange	ferric oxide and manganese dioxide
Yellow	1. silver chloride 2. sulfur in the form of sodium sulfide or potassium sulfide 3. carbon in the form of wood or charred horn
Greenish-yellow	uranium oxide
Green	1. ferrous oxide in the form of iron filing 2. cupric (blue) and ferric (yellow) oxides in the form of copper and iron filings
Black	manganese and iron oxide in large quantity
White, opal, or milk White, translucent	1. cryolite or fluorite and feldspar 2 calcium phosphate in the form of bone ash 3. tin or zinc oxides in large amounts
Turquoise	calcium phosphate, arsenic, and calcined brass dust (copper and tin oxides)

HOW TO TELL IF YOUR GLASS SLIPPER IS OLD

Anyone who says, "I can always tell when a shoe is 'old,'" has been fooled and does not know it. Even people who have access to expert opinion may be misled on the age or the maker of a particular shoe.

The chance that you may buy a shoe as an antique when it is not, is a fact of life. There is no foolproof method of authenticating glass. Some glass shoes can be dated by the maker, patent date, or a registration mark. The only way a collector can be prepared to recognize shoes and determine their age is to study original, authenticated shoes that are made of glass, pottery, or porcelain. The quality of glass, the patterns, styles, shapes, and methods of manufacture are important factors. Antique glass is a better quality of glass than glass produced during the Depression years and years when the cost determines the quality. Some patterns on older shoes are sharp, clear, and have a certain sheen when compared to new shoes. The new shoes have patterns that are not as sharp or distinct and have a crinkly look. The weight of glass in an older shoe is heavier, compared with the same style in a new shoe.

The colors used during the Victorian era were almost always restricted to blue, amber, crystal, canary yellow, pale green, milk white, and cranberry in England. As technology improved, the colors of glass have expanded to every color and combination imaginable.

Some collectors compare two shoes, using one old and one new of the same color, size, style, and pattern and have found the new shoe to be slightly smaller. This is not foolproof. It has been stated that a reproduction from a slightly larger mould could produce a shoe the same size as the older one.

If a glass shoe passes all of the tests of pattern, style, marks or patent dates, color, weight, and method of manufacture, the final and crucial examination involves the signs of wear. Signs of wear help to authenticate age.

Older glass shoes show signs of wear and scrapes and scratches of different depths on different parts of the surface. Household dust is filled with abrasive particles which cause wear marks that cannot be duplicated. When these marks are looked at under magnification, the small scratches, some in a different width, depth, and length can be seen. Scratches and wear marks can and do show up almost on all of the surfaces of old glass shoes. The scratches should be of little concern; when they are not seen, be cautious.

When determining the age of a porcelain or pottery shoe, the mark is the first thing to look for. While looking at the mark, check the quality of the paste; older porcelain is fine-grained, uniform in color, and reasonably free from defects. The glaze on older shoes is usually transparent and evenly applied. The style of the shoe or pattern can determine the age and quality. The last and important factor in determining the age of the shoe is the decoration, which includes the designs, combination of colors, and application of gilding. In most instances, new gilding is thinly applied using 14K; the older gilding is 22K and heavily applied. We know that hand-painted porcelain shoes were the fad in the years 1890 to 1915. During this Victorian-influenced period, it was considered lady-like to hand paint porcelain. To determine if the shoe is hand painted, use a 10X magnifying glass, and a smooth flowing design will be seen. Decals and transfer printing as decoration are an inexpensive substitute for hand-painted decoration. This style of decoration is sometimes difficult to detect, but if a 10X magnifying glass is used, one will see tiny dots making up the design, rather than the smooth flow of the hand-painted design. Transfer printing on porcelain is an economical method of decorating porcelain.

As Harold Peterson, said in his book *How Do You Know It's Old*, "Don't be ashamed of discovering you have been fooled, you are in the very best company." Know what is old by knowing what is new!

MILK GLASS SHOES

The popularity of milk glass proved profitable for companies to produce novelties such as slippers. This glass was called opal ware by early glassmakers and later was called milk glass because it resembled milk. In the mid 1800s, the popularity of milk glass reached its peak in America.

Milk glass is easy to recognize but difficult to date, unless the slipper has a registry mark or a manufacturer's date.

Some authors believe the nineteenth century milk glass is heavier, has a less oily texture, and translucency which can be seen when held to the light. (This is not to be confused with opalescent white glass.) These same authors stated that the reproductions are whiter, so much so

that it is almost a dead-white, denser and lighter in weight.

The recognition of the age is important but so is recognition of some well-known companies, such as Sowerby's, Ellison Glassworks, Henry Greener & Company, and George Davidson & Company of England. The Vallerysthal glass factory of France produced milk glass shoes and other wares until 1930 when the factory was destroyed. We see many of the shoes marked "France," "Made in France," and "Lancome" that are collectible.

Several American companies produced milk glass slippers and a few companies are continuing to reproduce quality slippers, boots, and shoes.

DEPRESSION ERA GLASS SHOES

According to Weatherman (1970), Depression glass was the relatively inexpensive glassware which is recognized as that which was made in colors, primarily by machine, and sold or given away during (or very near) the years of the Great Depression.

During the Depression (1920 – 1940), few Americans had the money to buy glass shoes that were nonfunctional and purely decorative. However, the shelves of many homes were brightened during this bleak time with colorful glass shoes. The Depression hit the glass factories as hard as other industries, but glass was machine-pressed in large quantities at a cost that was low enough to allow some Americans to buy and for some merchants to give as promotional items.

It was during this time that old moulds were used with less glass or a poorer quality. The sharpness of some designs and patterns is lacking and in some cases dull and crinkly. Very clearly, by comparing shoes, the differences will be evident.

GLASS CATALOGS

Butler Brothers acted as distributors for glass companies and sent catalogs to all the major cities in the United States. These catalogs allowed manufacturers of glass, who wished to distribute their wares as widely as possible, to use Butler Brothers as an outlet.

After looking through the Butler Brothers catalog, it is evident that the greatest quantity of pressed glass was made and sold between 1880 and 1910. While these catalogs served the purpose of showing what was available to be bought at wholesale, there was a lack of information concerning the actual manufacturer.

Some companies produced their own catalogs to advertise their wares to the local merchants but used Butler to assist in wider distribution and sales.

Collectors can only attribute any glass shoe to a specific place or manufacturer, unless the glass is marked with a sign or symbol of the maker.

The copy of the Butler Brothers catalog is a courtesy of the Smithsonian Museum.

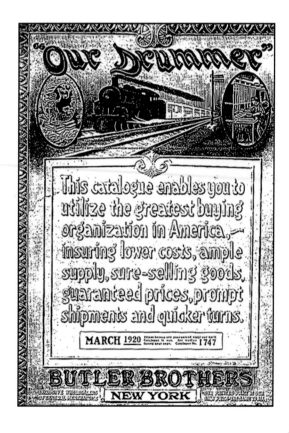

PATENTS AND PATTERNS

Peterson, in his book, *Glass Patents and Patterns*, stated that after 1861, patents were granted for 3½, 7, or 14 years for designs, and 17 years for inventions. United States patents have been issued since 1791 for inventions and since 1842 for designs. The present numbering system began in 1836, and the first patent was issued in 1842. Patents prior to July 1836 bear no official number. The Patent Act of 1842 required the owner of a patent to mark his article as patented and to include the date the patent was issued.

It is believed that some glassmakers still rely increasingly on the initiative of our ancestors. They make reproductions with long-expired patent dates. The words "Patent Applied For" or "Patent Pending" have no legal effect and little historical significance. Since the United States did not grant design patents until 1842, it is improbable that American glass made before that year would be marked with "Patent Applied For" or "Patent Pending." There were very few design patents on glassware until the 1860s.

Because information is fragmented and scanty, it is almost impossible to know when the actual production of shoes and slippers began and which companies produced and reproduced them. With so many companies, patterns, and styles to keep track of, the beginning collector and the inexperienced dealer may have difficulty distinguishing between glass slippers and shoes made in the 1800s and those made in the 1930s, and maybe even those made in the 1990s. This is due to the use of old moulds whose patents have expired.

ASSIGNMENTS OF PATENTS

Innes, in *Pittsburgh Glass, 1797 – 1891: A History and Guide for Collectors*, stated that what started out as a novelty in 1876 was a sideline product ten years later. This is evident by the number of glass slippers made; practically all of the American glass factories produced them.

Slippers were so popular during the late 1800s that several glass designers and manufacturers had them registered with the patent office, whose records indicated that the patents were granted for 3½ years. Albert C. Revi, in his book, *American Pressed Glass and Figural Bottles*, stated that the following men obtained patent designs for slippers and shoes to be made from glass:

1. William L. Libbey patented a glass shoe on March 23, 1875, for the New England Glass Company.

2. Daniel R. Bradley of New York City filed an application on April 30, 1885, for a perfumery bottle, patent 16,181. It was granted on July 28, 1885.

3. Washington Beck patented a mould for "Daisy and Button" hanging slipper, June 13, 1886.

4. Washington Beck patented a mould for the manufacture of a glass shoe on July 11, 1886.

5. John E. Miller patented a glass slipper (The Daisy Miller) on October 19,1886.

6. Henry J. Smith patented a stubby toe slipper on October 19, 1886.

7. Herman Tappan applied for a patent on September 25, 1886, serial #214,569. His shoe patent was granted December 14, 1886.

8. Charles L. Fluccus of Pittsburgh, Pennsylvania, filed an application on January 24, 1890, serial #388,014. The patent for his first boot-shaped bottle, patent #19,669, was granted February 25, 1890.

9. James H. Hurlbut and George W. Bean patented their design for a bottle holder in the form of a high-buttoned shoe resting on a rounded base on March 8, 1887. The letters "B & H" appear in a circle on the base.

Note: William Butler patented a method for flashing color on blown and pressed glass on September 29, 1891.

THE DAISY AND BUTTON SLIPPERS

The Daisy and Button slipper/shoe is one of the most popular patterns. Collectors are grateful for clarification of the differences between slippers produced in the Daisy and Button pattern. According to Innes in *Pittsburgh Glass, 1979 – 1891*, John Ernest Miller of George Duncan & Sons of Pittsburgh patented a method of producing glass slippers. Mr. Miller assigned the rights to his patent to Duncan & Sons and Bryce Brothers. His patent #351,197 was granted October 19, 1886, the same day that Henry J. Smith of Pittsburgh was granted patent #351,216 for pressing slippers. Smith assigned his patent rights to George Duncan and Bryce Brothers also. Their processes for methods were similar.

Miller's method was to press the shoe into a mould and leave a separation almost to the toe, leaving the sides of the vamp upright. A "last" was inserted while the glass was pliable, and the open sides of the vamp were bent over the "last" to shape the shoe. The "last" was removed after the shoe cooled, producing an open slipper.

Revi defined a "last" as a block or form shaped like a human foot, over which shoe uppers are drawn and lasted.

Smith's method was to press his slipper with the toe folded up to meet the vamp, forming a stubby toe.

Duncan slippers were produced in blue, vaseline, crystal, and occasionally some were ruby-stained. Bryce slippers were produced in amber, crystal, and various shades of blue.

Confusion arises when collectors find the same patent date on the Duncan and Bryce slippers. Bredehoft et al, in their book *Early Duncan Glassware*, clarify the same patent date by explaining how to look at the patent dates and recognize the difference between Duncan and Bryce slippers. The patent date on the Duncan slipper, PAT Oct 19/86, is read by holding the slipper with the heel in the left hand and looking up through the sole — the date is inside the slipper. The patent date on the Bryce slipper, PATD Oct. 19, 1886, is read by holding the slipper vertically with the toe uppermost. The date appears across the arch of the underside of the slipper.

The patent dates may not be found in some of these old slippers because they were made earlier than the 1886 date and were listed in their own trade catalogs and other glass catalogs two years earlier.

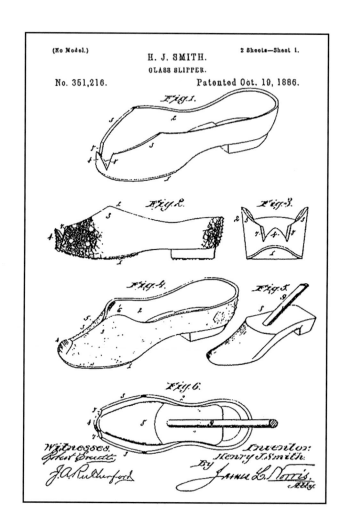

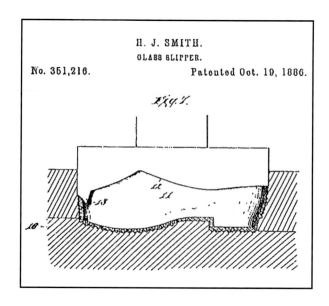

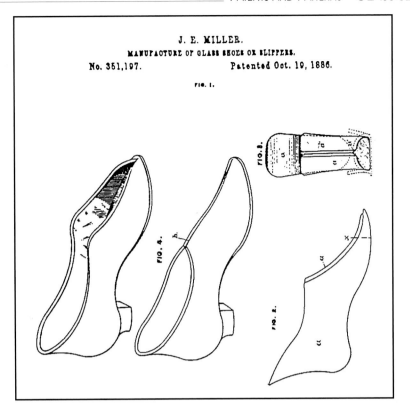

J. E. MILLER.
MANUFACTURE OF GLASS SHOES OR SLIPPERS.
No. 351,197.   Patented Oct. 19, 1886.

BOUQUET HOLDER

Herman Tappan of New York City was issued a patent on December 14, 1886, for a bouquet holder. This shoe rests on a fiddle-shaped base with two ribbon-shaped bands on the base with "Bouquet Holder" and the patent date 1886 or "Patent Pending" on the bottom. Fenton reintroduced and reproduced in 1965 and 1966 without any information on the base. (See the example at the top of page 83.)

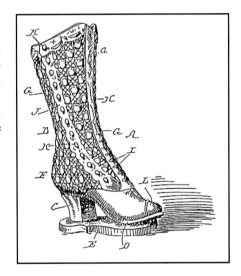

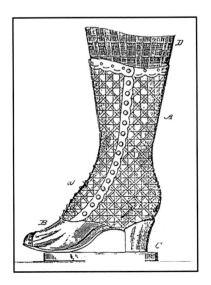

BOTTLE HOLDER

James H. Hurlbut and George W. Bean patented their design for a bottle holder in the form of a high-buttoned shoe resting on a base on March 8, 1887. The letters "B&H" appear in a circle on the base. This bottle holder was made with buttons on the right and left. The Bellaire Goblet Company of Findlay, Ohio, made this in crystal, amber, vaseline, and blue.

GLASS SLIPPERS
AND SHOES

The large green Daisy and Button slipper, 11½" x 4½" x 2½" has the design all over, including the sole and heel. $150.00 – 165.00. A shoe with Daisy and Button pattern on the sole and plain sides is discussed by Lee plate #206. This slipper is pictured on page 85 of Albert C. Revi's book, *American Pressed Glass and Figural Bottles* and has been attributed to Bryce Brothers. No one has emphatically stated who made this slipper. $165.00 – 185.00.

Three novelty slippers, 2¼" x 1¼", were described by Ruth Lee as thimble holders, made for the Pan American Exposition at Buffalo, New York, in 1901. **Left** — a pale green. **Middle** — green. **Right** — amethyst. Lee plate #183. $150.00 – 165.00 ea.

Left — A frosted or satin slipper, 4⅞" x 2¾". The large bow is in front of the slightly turned-up pointed toe. Embossed on the back above the heel is "Worlds Fair – 1893." On the sole is "Libbey Glass Co. Toledo, Ohio." Lee plate #195. $95.00. Libbey built an exhibition factory on the Columbian Exposition Fairgrounds in Chicago, Illinois. **Right** — A frosted slipper, 5⅛" x 2¾", has a solid heel and

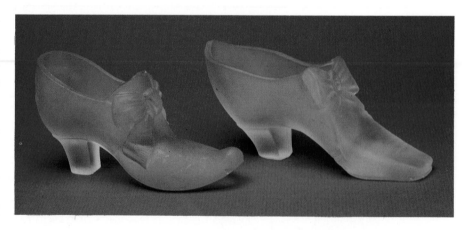

hollow depression under the sole of the square toe. Marked "Gillinder & Sons Centennial Exposition 1876." $100.00. They set up a combination exhibition factory, showroom, and sales office on the Centennial Exposition grounds in Philadelphia where visitors could actually see the glass being made and could purchase some if they wished. Lee plate #199.

An amber covered boot, 3¾" x 1⅞". The cover has an embossed design. Circa 1910. $65.00.

Left — a small crystal shoe bottle, 3½" x ⅞", with bow on the vamp. $50.00.
Middle — crystal ladies' boot, 3¼" x 4¼", with buttons down the side. $50.00.
Right — same as the left, except there is a flower on the vamp rather than a bow. $50.00. All circa 1900. Lee plate #182.

Left — crystal blown glass shoe bottle, 5¼" x 1⅝", with a bow at the vamp and under the sole the number "27" in a circle. Lee plate #183. Circa 1890. **Right** — shoe bottle, 4" x 1⅝" with flowers on the vamp. Lee plate #183. $75.00 ea.

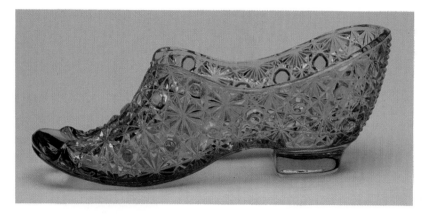

The amber Daisy and Button slipper, 7¼" x 1¾", was made by Bryce Bros. of Pittsburgh. It has a ribbed toe and a panel of horizontal ribbing over the heel. Lee plate #196. Circa 1886. $60.00 – 65.00.

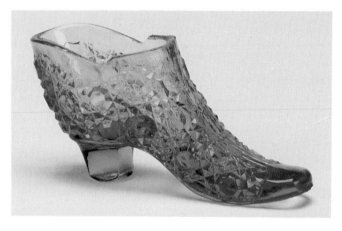

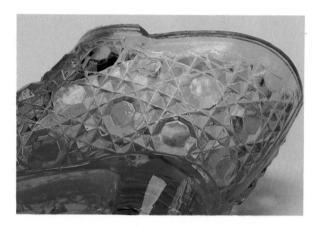

Close-up to show the cane pattern.

The blue, high cut slipper in the cane pattern, 4¾" x 2¼", has a fine mesh on the sole. Note the plain panel that runs from the toe up the front of the slipper. Lee states that the slipper was produced by the United Stated Glass Company. Also available in amber and crystal. Lee plate #202. Circa 1880. $60.00 – 75.00.

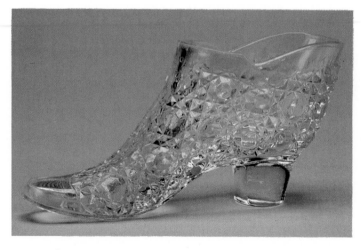

Crystal, same as the slipper shown above.

Crystal slipper on skates, 4" x 2¾", in the Daisy and Button pattern. It has a mesh sole, a plain toe, and a plain panel that runs from the toe to the top of the slipper. The edge of the top is a border formed of scallops. Lee plate #202. Circa 1880. $60.00 – 75.00.

A pair of attached crystal slippers, 2¾" l x 1¼" h x 2" w. There is a round depression for salt. Lee plate #199. Circa 1900. $65.00.

The dark amber slipper, approximately 5" long, according to the dealer was made around the 1920s and was used as a pipe holder. The design is simple and resembles a man's slipper. $40.00.

The blue round covered boot on a round base has a star ornamented cover. $80.00 – 100.00. Lee plate #194, stated that it was illustrated in a Butler Bros. catalog of the 1800s as "our funny ink stand." This advertisement read that it was made in an artistic manner in assorted colors to be sold for ten cents! These boots were also made without covers for matches, as the amber one on the right. According to Kamm, Bryce Higbee & Co. of Pittsburgh, Pennsylvania, in 1887 produced the utility ink well and utility toothpick holder that some catalogs called the "Rip Van Winkle" boot.

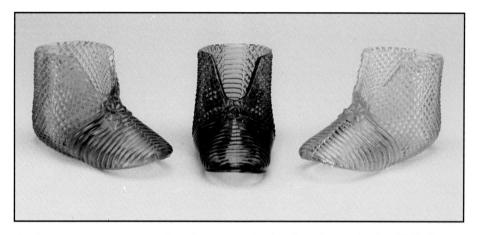

Amber, sea green, and pale green baby bootees, 4⅛" x 2½", have ribbed vamps with two flowers. Most of the bootee has the fine diamond pattern and has a hollow toe. The third bootee is pale green. Lee plate #196. Circa 1890. $75.00 – 90.00.

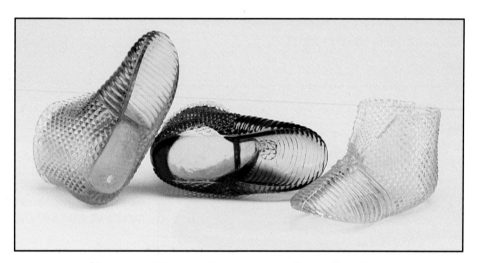

Close-up of the bootees to show the hollow toes.

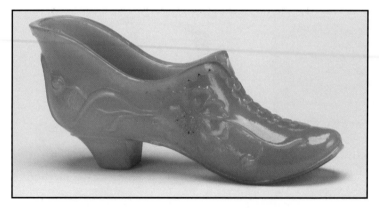

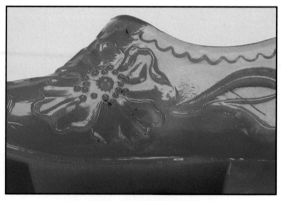

The opaque light blue slipper, 4¾" x 2¼" long, has poppy decoration in relief on the sides, and it is laced up the front and gilded. Only slight traces of the gilding remain. Lee plate #199. Circa 1890. $65.00 – 80.00.

Close-up of the light blue slipper.

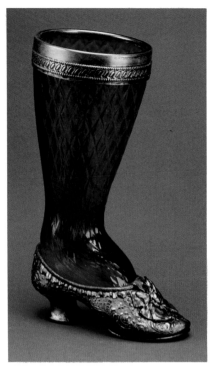

Left — a fine diamond mesh 3" x 4" shoe on skates designed with a flared top and a scalloped edge. The shoe section is meant to simulate alligator, but the toe is plain. Lee plate #194. Circa 1910. $50.00. **Right** — horizontal ribbing all over the 4¼" h x 3¾" l high shoe. It has a solid Cuban heel and a hollow space under the foot. Lee plate #198. $75.00.

The large cranberry leg, 10½", in a Victorian pewter slipper, 6" x 2", is one of the most beautiful pewter slippers ever made. Circa 1870, from England. $750.00 – 850.00. Cranberry glass had its hey-day during the Victorian era and was popular for so long that collectors from all walks of life and coast-to-coast sought and bought it.

Dense amber "three-way" heavy shoes, 4½" x 4⅜", in finecut pattern. The base is stippled in a triangle that accommodates each shoe. Made by the Belliare Goblet Company of Findlay, Ohio. Circa 1800. Lee plate #194. $200.00 – 225.00.

Blue finecut pattern slipper, 5½" x 3½", on skates. The front is opened into a "V" and filled in. The toe is plain with eyelets to lace up the "V." Lee plate #197. $75.00 – 90.00.

A pair of salt and pepper shakers 4" high with pewter tops. Each boot is decorated with a shield on a rayed base. Circa 1876. Lee #189. $100.00 pair.

Pair of salt and pepper shakers on a shell base. $100.00 pair.

Amber boot, 2" x 3¼", with a band of horizontal ribs as decoration just above the instep. Circa 1800. Lee plate #188. $50.00 – 65.00.

Amber Daisy and Button slipper, 5¼" x 3¼", on skates is high in front, has a plain toe, and a plain band around the top. Circa 1800. Lee plate #197. $75.00 – 85.00.

Amber Chinese-type shoe, 5⅛" x 2¼", on a toboggan. The bottom of the toboggan has a pair of snowshoes as decoration, the front of the toboggan has a smaller pair. Ruth L. Webb believed these to be made by Bryce Brothers of Pittsburgh, Pennsylvania. Lee plate #196. $125.00 – 150.00.

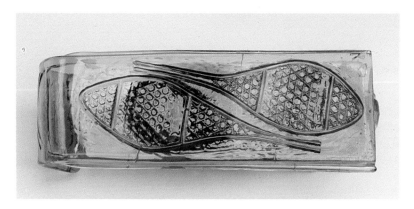

The bottom of the toboggan.

Four Chinese-type shoes in the cane pattern, blue, canary, crystal, or amber. Each measuring 4¾" x 1¾". Circa 1880. Lee plate #202. $75.00 – 90.00 ea.

Green satin oxford, 2¼" x 1¾", has exceptionally fine details and four laces. Circa 1890. Lee plate #183. $150.00 – 165.00.

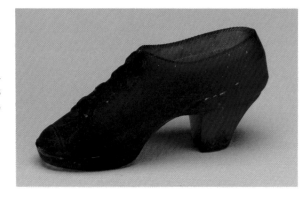

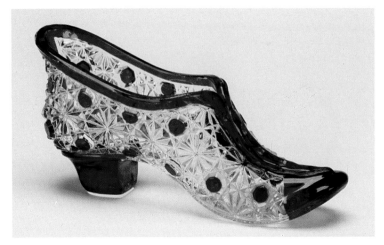

Duncan crystal shoe, 4¾" x 2½", with ruby stained buttons, heel and toe and a mesh sole. Marked "PATD OCT. 19/86." Lee plate #198. $100.00.

Blue Daisy and Button sandal, 4½" x 1⅜", was also made in amethyst and vaseline. Circa 1880. Lee plate #202. $85.00.

Amber example of the previous sandal. $85.00.

Green and white spatter glass boot, 5½" x 3", has applied crystal leaf on the vamp and riga-ree around the top. Circa 1900. Lee plate #181. $125.00 – 150.00.

Dark red spatter glass boot, 5" x 3¾", $125.00 – 150.00.

Heavy hollow slipper with a pointed toe that is turned up. A small bow in front and a row of beading forms a border around the edge. Circa 1886. Lee plate #194. $85.00 – 100.00.

The front of the left slipper.

Crystal slipper, 4¾" x 2⅜", has a British Registry Mark, ®^{d} #87058, and a peacock head inside denoting that it was produced by Sowerby's of Gateshead on Tyne, England. Sowerby registered their design in London on November 15, 1887, and produced it in several colors and in slag. $75.00.

Amber Diamond pattern slipper, 5⅛" x 2½", has a flat bow and a slightly squared toe. The bow is stippled and the ribbon ends hang down almost to the toe. Circa 1890. Lee plate #202. $75.00.

Close-up to show the pattern.

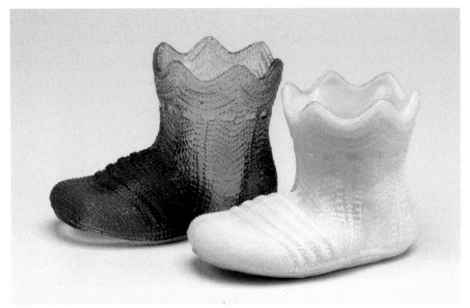

Amber and opaque light blue baby bootees, 2½" x 3½". Lee, in plate #188, describes the detail as "fine and lacy," and resembling a knitted baby's bootee. Produced by the King Glass Company, Pittsburgh, Pennsylvania, 1880. These bootees were produced in amber, opaque light blue, apple green, clear blue, and crystal. $100.00 – 125.00.

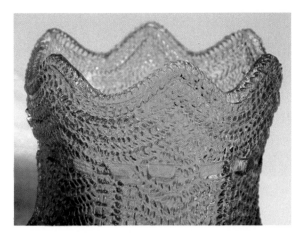

Close-up of the opaque blue to show the pattern on the foot portion.

Close-up of the amber to show the top of the bootee.

Three small shoes, 3" x 1½", in the Diamond pattern with steps that once held small bottles. **Left** – peach, has a tiny paper label marked "Lancome France." $35.00. **Middle** – amber. $25.00. **Right** – amethyst. $25.00.

Three varying sizes of amber fine cut or Diamond Block patterns are opened into a filled-in "V." They are laced up to the "V," the toe is plain, the front of the sole is treaded. **Left** — 5⅞" x 3⅛". $65.00. **Middle** — 5¼" x 2¾". $55.00. **Right** — 4" x 2¼". $55.00. Circa 1890.

Three varying sizes of blue fine cut or Diamond. (Same values as above.)

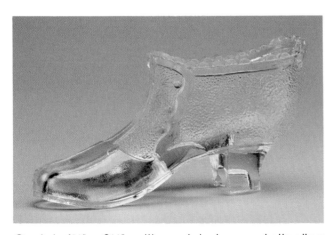

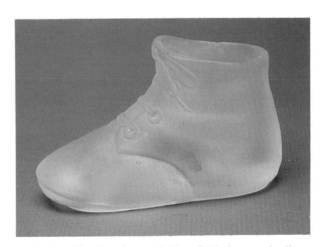

Crystal, 4¾" x 2¼", with a plain toe and stippling over the rest of the shoe. It has six buttons closing the shoe. There is a hollow sole and an indented heel. Circa 1900. $65.00.

A frosted baby shoe, 3⅛" x 2⅛", has a hollow sole. The laces close the shoe. Circa 1930. Lee plate #190. $50.00.

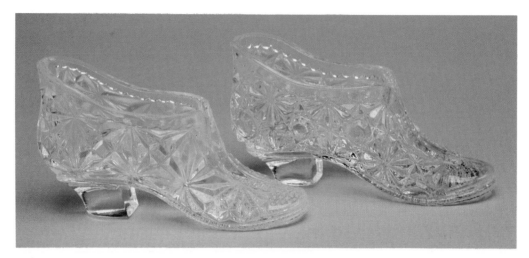

Left — soft lemon color Daisy and Square stubby slipper, 3¼" x 2½", with solid toe was made by Duncan. $30.00. N. Bredehoft et al in their book *Early Duncan Glassware*, p. 152, referred to it as #3. Circa 1890. **Right** — crystal shoe, 3¼" x 3½", in the Daisy and Button pattern is slightly narrower than the yellow Duncan. $20.00.

Close-up of yellow to show pattern.

Green, 4½" x 2½", plain except for a scalloped border near the edge and double lines on the vamp. It has a hollow sole and solid heel. Circa 1920. Lee plate #193. $65.00 – 75.00.

Crystal, 7½" x 3½", plain toe and Sunburst pattern, Bull's Eye center, a row of hobnails form a border around the edge. There is a flat bow in front. The sole and the heel are indented. Produced by Sowerby. Circa 1880. Lee plate #195. $65.00 – 75.00.

Three high shoes, 4" x 5½", cane pattern mounted on a scroll fiddle-shaped base. The patent for the boot bouquet holders was granted to Herman Tappan of New York City on December 14, 1886. The design number given to Mr. Tappan was #17, 023. **Left** — blue with wording "Bouquet Holder" on one side of the base. "Patented Dec. 1886" on th other side of the base. $100.00. **Middle** — amber shoe has the wording "Bouquet Holder" on one side of the base and "Patent Applied For" on the other side. $65.00. **Right** — yellow, has the same wording as the left. Lee plate #201. $100.00.

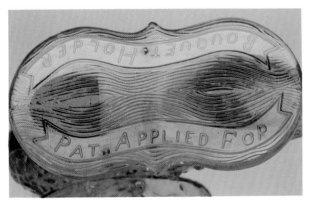

The bottom of the base to show "Patent Applied For."

The bottom of the base to show patented shoe from above.

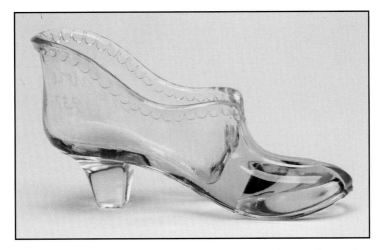

Pale green, 4¾" x 2¾", has a row of scallops along the edge, solid heel, and hollow sole. Circa 1900. Lee plate #192. $60.00 – 75.00.

The black boot*, 4" x 3¼", is cuffed and has a clearly defined spur. The sole is solid. Circa 1900. Lee plate #201. $75.00.

The bottom to show solid heel of the black boot. *When held to bright sunlight shows dark amethyst.

Flashed red, 4½" x 2½", scalloped border near the edge and double lines on the vamp. It has a hollow sole, solid heel, and the gilded name of city (souvenir item). Circa 1920. $75.00 – 85.00.

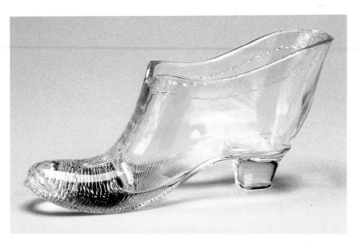

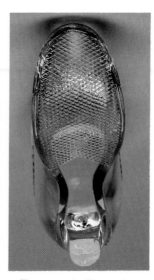

Crystal, 4¼" x 3", has six holes for laces and a scalloped edge around the entire top of the slipper. The sole has a mesh-like design. Circa 1900. $85.00 – 95.00.

Front view of the crystal shoe.

The mesh-like sole.

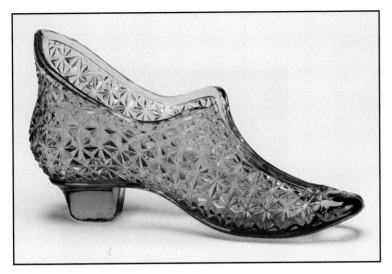

Amber fine cut pattern, 5¾" x 3¼", laces to a "V" at the top. The plain toe tilts upward. Produced in crystal, yellow, amber, and blue. Circa 1890. Lee plate #202. $75.00.

Close-up of fine cut pattern.

Stippled, 4½" x 2½", with a small bow and Cuban heel. Circa 1930. Lee plate #192. $50.00. This slipper was reproduced and re-introduced during the 1960s.

The vaseline high shoe, 4" x 5½", flower holder is mounted on a scalloped base. The base is marked "B.H." Circa 1890. Lee plate #193. $100.00. (Accidentally dropped during the photography and the base chipped.)

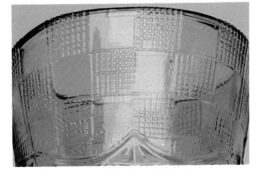

The top of the boot is shown.

Blue crystal shoe skate, 4½" high, in the diamond block pattern. In the scalloped edge on the side is a patent date of December, 1886. $100.00.

Close-up of the shoe skate showing the date.

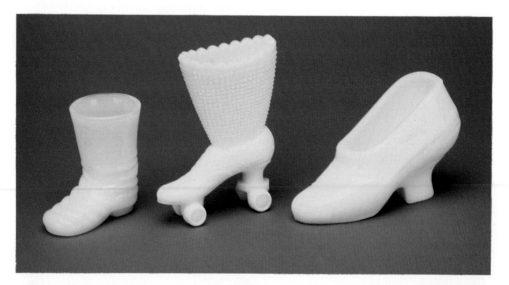

Left — white milk glass wrinkled boot, 2¾" x 2¾". Lee plate #190. $45.00. This boot was reproduced and re-introduced by Degenhart Crystal Art Glass Company, Boyd Art Glass Company, and I have seen a boot marked "Japan." **Middle** — shoe skate, 3¼" x 3⅞". The shoe section simulates alligator. The flared top has a fine cut design. The sole has a fine diamond pattern, between the skates the word "France." $55.00. **Right** — heavy slipper, 4¾" x 3", has a row of beading across the toe and around the entire shoe. It has a squatty heel. $50.00. Lee plate #200. This slipper was reproduced and re-introduced, 1960 – 1965.

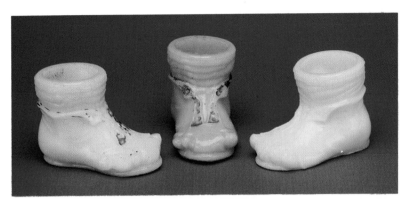

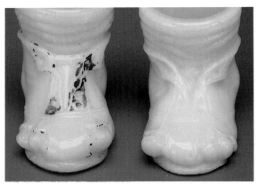

Three ragged hobo, tramp, or baby shoes, 2⅞" x 2", toes protruding through the end. **Left** — right great toe protruding, traces of gold, and an oblong indentation under the sole, circa 1901. $75.00. **Middle** — lavender, same as left. $75.00. **Right** — the left great toe protruding. The indentation under the sole is round. Circa 1901. $85.00. Lee plate #193.

Close-up of toes from above.

Condiment holder, 6" x 3", cut in old block pattern, according to Swan (1986) in her book, *American Cut and Engraved Glass of the Brilliant Period*, p. 128. "The slipper was probably made or cut by Mt. Washington Glass Company or Smith Brothers of New England Glass Company." This shoe was bought at an antique auction in Laguna Beach, California. $250.00 – 300.00.

Another view of the shoe, showing the mustard jar and salt and pepper shakers. Circa 1894.

Men's blue boot, 4" x 3⅛", with horizontal ribbing on the heel. The vamp is stippled and the back of the boot is plain. Circa 1886. Lee plate #193. $80.00.

Men's black boot, same as the previous one except for inscription. $75.00.

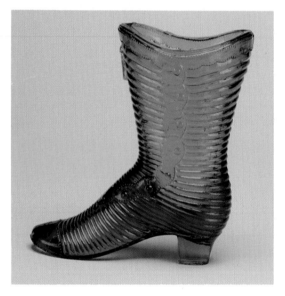

Amber high shoe, 4¼" x 3¾", horizontal ribbing, solid Cuban heel, and hollow space under foot. Lee plate #198. $60.00.

Crystal pair of attached baby shoes, 3⅛" x 2". Listed as a "double shoe." Made by the King Glass Company, Pittsburgh, Pennsylvania, in blue, dark amber, and light amber. Circa 1880. Lee plate #196. $145.00.

Left — pale blue 2" x ¾" spun glass slipper trimmed with a yellow band of glass around the top forming a bow. **Right** — the same as the left except for the trim in green and a darker blue. Circa 1920. $45.00 ea.

Pale green boot, 3" x 5½", blown glass decorated with a painted scene in the front. Circa 1900. $55.00.

Most of the advertising on the pressed glass slippers is pressed into the sole. A method of forming letters on glass was patented by William H. Maxwell of Pittsburgh, Pennsylvania, on March 22, 1887. The letters and numbers were simply pressed into the surface of the glass. The lettering that is part of the mould was limited to a particular region or manufacturer for the sole purpose of advertisement. Revi remarked that these slippers were "made-to-order" for shops as "give-aways" to be given to customers and friends. Pictured are Daisy & Button slippers, which were made by George Duncan & Sons and Bryce Brothers, with the following nine advertisements. The value of each is $125.00 – 150.00.

Blue Duncan slipper, 5" x 2¼", on the sole "J.C. Brandt Saint Louis Pat. Oct. 19/86."

Amber Duncan slipper, 6" x 2⅞", on the sole "S.D. Sollers & Co. Fine Shoes."

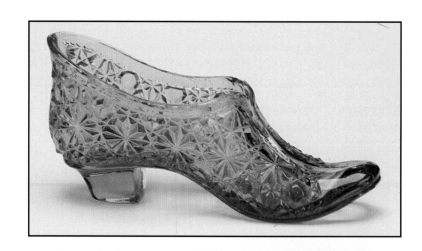

Amber Duncan slipper, 5" x 2¼", on the sole "Brown Brothers, Oct. 19/86."

Crystal Bryce slipper, 4¾" x 1¾", on the sole "Michaelsons."

Yellow Duncan slipper, 5⅞" x 2⅞", with an open toe and on the sole "KASTS."

Crystal Bryce slipper, 4¾" x 1¾", on the sole "Meis Store."

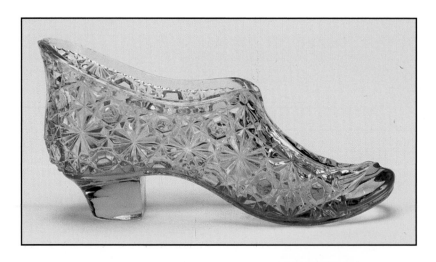

Blue Duncan slipper, 5" x 2¼", on the sole "Sollers & Co. No 18N8, hst."

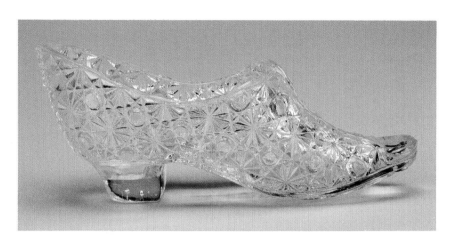

Crystal Bryce slipper, 4⅞" x 1⅞", on the sole "Fontius."

Crystal Duncan slipper, 6" x 2⅞", on the sole "Crystal Slipper."

Large pale blue Dutch style, 8¼" x 3". Has the traces and remains of a lid that was removed because of a large crack. $50.00.

A crystal slipper in the Daisy and Button pattern with a bow that has three distinct lines across it. The pattern is a sharp, deep design. This slipper has a light tint of purple that occurs when crystal with a slight amount of magnesium is exposed to the sun. This was reported by the dealer to be a Cambridge slipper, circa 1910. $85.00.

The front to show the bow.

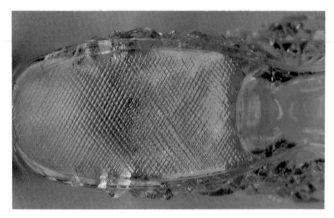

The sole to show the tread bottom.

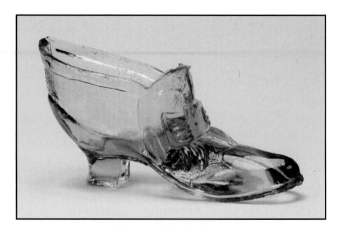

Amber slipper, 4¾" x 2½", with stippling on the upper part of the back of the shoe and under the bow in front. It has a hollow sole with an indented heel. From England. $70.00 – 80.00.

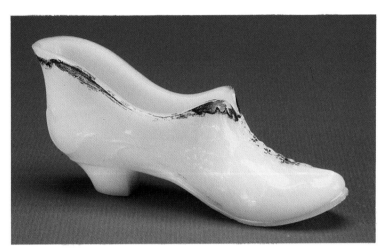

Milk glass cat in shoe, painted with gold, 4" x 3½", with the name of a town. $65.00 – 75.00. The small bow around the neck of the cat was lost. This shoe was featured in the Butler Bros. catalog, April 1906.

White milk glass shoe, 5" x 2⅛", with traces of gold, the relief or embossed poppy and vine decorates both sides. Circa 1900. Lee plate #199. $65.00 – 75.00.

The Duncan slipper in Daisy and Button pattern, 5¾" x 3", marked "PATD Oct19/86" with a perfume bottle. $65.00 – 85.00.

The perfume bottle. $25.00 – 40.00.

Black, 4⅝" x 2½", has high vamp, stippled front and back, a row of beading forms the design across the toe. Hollow sole and indented heel. Circa 1880. Lee plate #193. From England. $75.00.

Close-up showing front.

Three wrinkled boots, 2¾" x 2¾", with a star under the heel. The amber has a personal "hello, Los Angeles 1936" etched across the toe. $35.00. The green and blue are etched with "Los Angeles 1936" across the foot section of the boot. Circa 1930. $35.00 – 45.00 each.

Ruby cocktail shaker, 15½" x 6¾", is a foot and leg decorated with silver. The chrome sandal is decorated (the straps across the toe and vamp are the makeup of the sandal). Circa 1930. $450.00 – 600.00. This decanter is pictured in G. Florence's book, *Kitchen Glassware of the Depression Years*. Ruth Lee discussed a similar boot in her *Victorian Glass* book, plate #186. A crystal cocktail shaker in the same shape of a foot and leg is owned by a collector in the Midwest.

Three crystal boots. **Left** — clear boot, 3" x 2½". $30.00. **Middle** — 3⅛" x 2¾". $15.00. **Right** — 2¾" x 2¾". $25.00. Circa 1930.

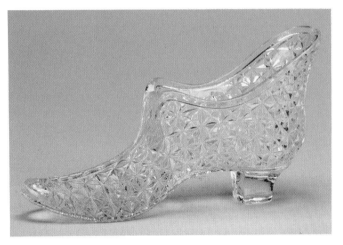

Fine cut crystal, 5¾" x 3⅛", laces to a "V" at the top. The toe is plain and tilts upward. Under the sole is "H.T." Circa 1880. This slipper was produced in yellow, amber, and blue; Lee plate #202. $75.00 – 85.00.

Close-up of the front.

The sole to show the "H.T."

Crystal cat slipper, 5⅞" x 3", has an alligator design on the entire front and Daisy, "no button," on the back. The fur on the cat is distinct and clear. Circa 1880. Lee plate #202. These slippers were made by the Columbia Glass Company, Findlay, Ohio, and continued by the U. S. Glass Company. $75.00 – 85.00.

Blue and amber Columbia cat slippers, same as above.

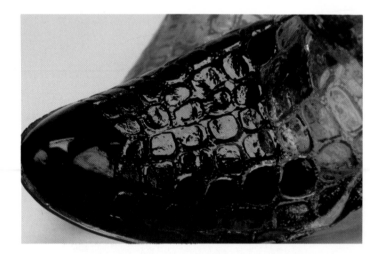

Close-up of the toe of the cat slippers.

Blue shoe on skates, 3" x 4", in a Diamond Mesh Pattern. The shoe section is meant to simulate alligator. There is a single row of beading around the top. The sole is covered with a Fine Diamond Pattern. Circa 1880. Lee plate #194. $50.00 – 60.00.

Men's black boot, 4" x 3⅛", with horizontal ribbing on the heel. The vamp is stippled, the top "M. Dawson – Trainer, J. Watts – Jockey"; in front "Lord Rosebery's Ladas, Winner of Derby – 1884." A boot with and without the inscription was possible by designing a mould with several side pieces to be inserted as required. $175.00 – 250.00.

The top of the boot.

An Example of Information Furnished by a Dealer

The dealer gave me a written statement at the time of purchase that confirmed the information that I later researched about the boot using Colin Lattimore's book *English Nineteenth Century Press – Moulded Glass*. The inscription commemorates the winning of the Derby in 1894 by Lord Rosebery's horse, Ladas. Around the top of the boot are the words, "M. Dawson – Trainer, J. Watts – Jockey." Across the instep these words: "Lord Rosebery's Ladas – Winner of Derby – 1894."

Black Glass Jockey's Boot.

4⅛" in length – 3⅛" high at the heel.
Marked around top band: "M.
Dawson – Trainer – J. Watts – Jockey".
Across the instep these words:
"Lord Rosebery's Ladas –
Winner of Derby – 1894."
From: "The Encyclopedia of
Sports" by Frank G. Menke
Published by A.S. Barnes and
Co., New York – Epsom Derby
at Epsom Downs, England –
Three year olds – 1 mile 885 yards.
Winner 1894 – Ladas – Owner
Lord Rosebery – Winner's Purse
$ 27,500."
Very rare.

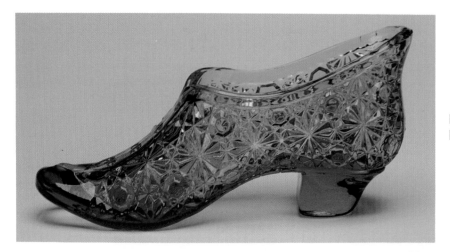

Blue Daisy and Button, 5" x 2½", Duncan slipper. $65.00 – 75.00.

"The patent date, 'PATD Oct 19.86,' is read by holding the slipper with the heel in the left hand and looking through the sole." Bredehoft et al.

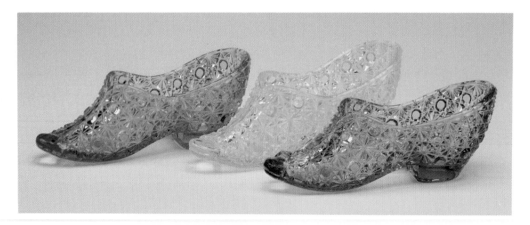

Blue, yellow, and amber Daisy and Button, 4⅝" x 1⅞", Bryce slippers. $65.00 – 75.00.

"The patent date, 'PATD Oct 19, 1886,' is read by holding the slipper vertically with the toe upper-most. The date appears across the arch of the shoe." Bredehoft et al.

Crystal slipper, 7⅛" x 1¾", in the Bryce Daisy and Button pattern over entire shoe and sole. The stubby toe is folded up, meeting the vamp of the shoe at the base of its fold. Marked "PATD Oct 19, 1886." $75.00 – 85.00.

Two crystal Bryce slippers. $75.00 – 85.00 ea.

The sole to show Daisy and Button pattern.

Blue Bryce Daisy and Button, same as above. $75.00 – 85.00.

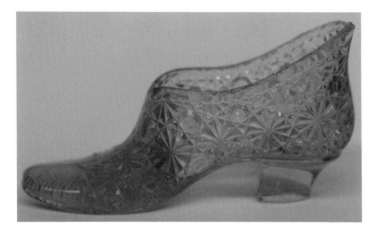

Blue Daisy and Button shoe, 4⅞" x 2½", resembles the Duncan shoe at first glance. It has the same four laces as the Duncan. The sole is solid with a mesh design. (The Duncan has a clear sole and is open to the toe.) Circa 1880. $75.00 – 85.00.

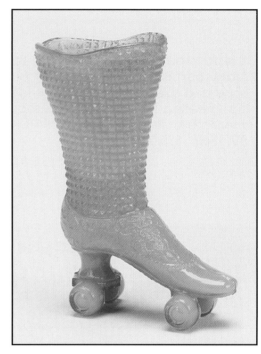

Blue shoe skate, 3⅜" l x 4¼" h, in Fine Diamond Mesh, does not have a scalloped edge. The flare is smaller than the shoe skate made by Central Glass Company, Sagamore, Massachusetts, reproduced and re-introduced in 1988. According to the company, the mold was purchased from Westmoreland Glass Co. of Pennsylvania, when the company went out of business in 1985. $50.00 – 65.00.

Left – pale green (same pattern as right). Guernsey shoe. $15.00. Guernsey Glass Co. of Cambridge, Ohio, uses the old Cambridge Triangle and a "B." Circa 1985. **Right** – canary yellow Daisy and Star in a Square. Duncan shoe, 3¼" x 1¾", circa 1880. $35.00. Note the back of both shoes.

Blue, 6" x 2½", with a clear band across the top, applied pink flowers decorating the front. The crystal heel has flecks of gold. $50.00 – 65.00.

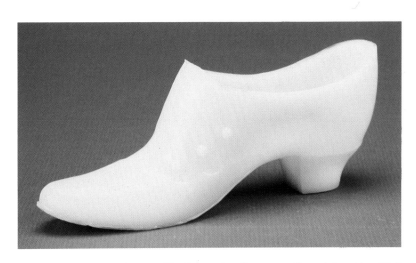

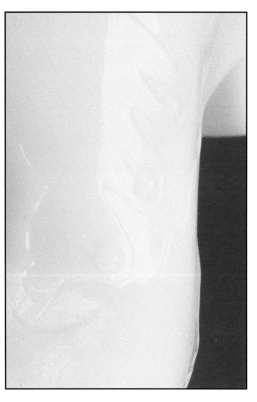

White milk glass shoe with three buttons on the side, 6" x 2⅛", has plain sole. Circa 1900. $75.00 – 85.00.

Close-up to show buttons.

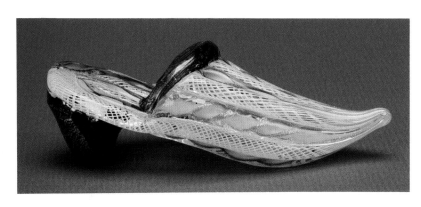

White latticing, 3¾" x 1⅝", with alternating yellow, pink, and blue decorating the entire slipper. $50.00 – 65.00.

Blue and white, 5¾" x 2¾", alternating latticing slipper with a crystal ruffle and heel. $50.00 – 65.00.

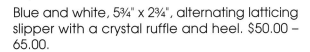

Blue and white 5⅛" x 2" millefiore with a crystal ruffle and heel. $35.00.

Miniature millefiore Murano slipper, 2¾" x ¾", blue and white on a red background. $35.00.

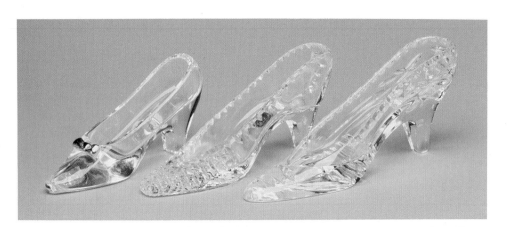

Left — crystal, 5" x 2¼", decorated with a small gold bow. Circa 1984. **Middle** — crystal, 6½" x 3", on paper label, "Georgian Crystal Tutbury LTD." Made in England. Circa 1986. **Right** — crystal, 7" x 3" on paper label, "Goldinger Crystal," hand molded. Made in Germany. Circa 1986. $25.00 ea.

Waterford baby bootee, 4⅛" x 2¼", paperweight. Circa 1986. $85.00.

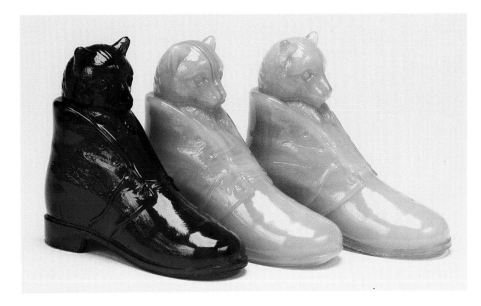

"Puss and Boots" with the tongue of the shoe hanging down the front. The Pairpoint Glass Co. of Sagamore, Massachusetts, reproduced and re-introduced these shoes in 1988. According to the company, the mold was purchased from Westmoreland Glass Co. of Pennsylvannia, when the company went out of business in 1985. **Left**: — cobalt blue, 4 x 3¾". **Middle** — pale blue opalescent. **Right** — lavender opalescent. $10.00 – 15.00 each.

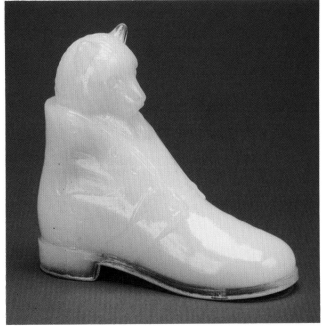

Pale yellow opalescent "Puss and Boots." $10.00 – 15.00 each.

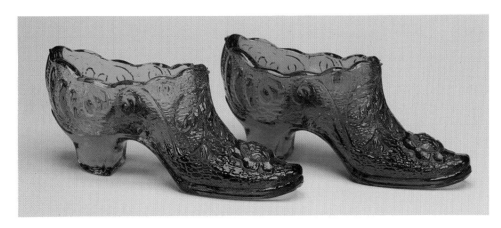

Amber and blue heavy shoes, 6" x 2½", with embossed flower. The top of the shoes are scalloped, made by Kanawaha Glass Co., West Virginia. Circa 1968. Kanawaha no longer exists — it was bought by Raymond Dereume Glass Inc. The new company still produces the colonial slipper. $15.00 – 18.00 each.

Green and blue Colonial bow (Cinderella) slippers, 5¾" x 2¼", were made by Kanawaha Glass Co., Dunbar, West Virginia. $20.00 – 30.00. The Degenhart Crystal Art Glass Company reproduced and re-introduced this slipper in 1947. Boyd Crystal Art Glass Co. produced the slipper using the Degenhart mould in 1978. The slippers can be easily identified by looking at the knot of the bow. Degenhart and Boyd have three distinct horizontal markings on the bow.

Close-up to show Kanawaha label.

Close-up of the bow.

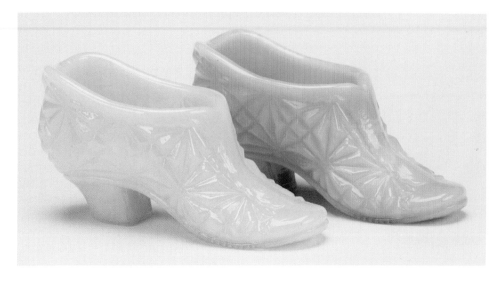

Small lavender and jade Daisy and Button shoes, 3⅛" x 1⅝", made by Guernsey Glass Co. of Cambridge, Ohio. Circa 1985. $10.00 – 15.00 set. Note the back of these shoes are lower than the Duncan shoe. They are marked with the old Cambridge triangle with a "B" inside the triangle.

The orange shoe, same as the lavender and jade shoes made by Guernsey Glass.

Golden amber Daisy & Square shoe on skates, 4¼" l x 3⅛" h. Close-up made by L.E. Smith Co. Circa 1978. See "Reproductions." $10.00 – 15.00.

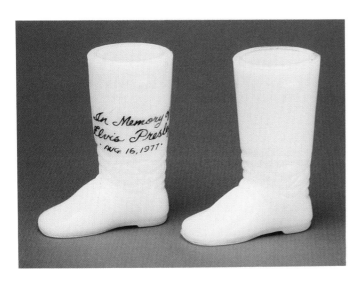

White milk glass boots made by Guernsey. **Left** — commemorates the life and death of Elvis Presley. **Right** — plain. Circa 1984. $15.00 – 20.00 ea.

Three boots, green, blue, and red, 3¼" x 4". $25.00 ea.

Three shoes, 5⅞" x 2¾", with the Daisy and Button pattern on the front of the shoes except the toes. The back of the shoes have the Daisy and Button pattern also. These shoes were made by L.E. Smith Glass Company, Mt. Pleasant, Pennsylvania. **Left** — amber, circa 1969. **Middle** — iridescent, circa 1974. **Right** — red, circa 1974. $15.00 – 18.00 ea.

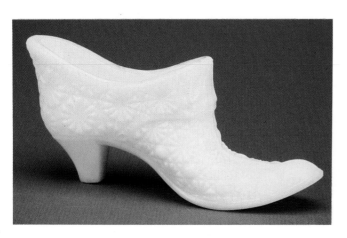

White milk glass shoe by L.E. Smith. $15.00 – 18.00.

Left — amethyst boot, 2½" x 2¾", has a slight turned toe (the dealer called it a Santa boot). $15.00 – 20.00. **Right** — cobalt blue boot, 1⅞" x 3", has an applied heel. Circa 1920. $30.00 – 40.00.

Left — pink boot, 2⅜" x 2½". Marked "France" on the sole. $15.00 – 20.00. **Right** — light blue, 2¾" x 2½". $10.00 – 15.00.

Yellow boot, 4¼" x 6½". Circa 1970. $10.00 – 15.00.

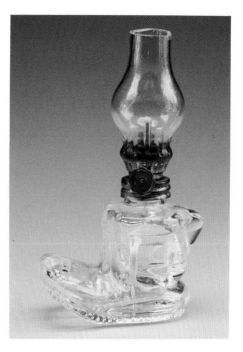

A crystal lamp shoe is 4" x 6½", circa 1985. $5.00.

Left — amber boot, 3" x 4", with a tiny lip for pouring. $8.00 – 10.00. **Right** — amber boot, 2¾" x 3½", has a spur intact. $10.00.

A heavy green boot, 7" x 10", with an applied handle and a western motif over the entire boot. Circa 1950. $35.00.

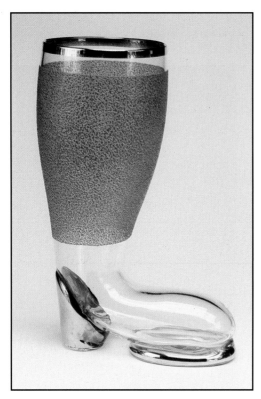

A martini boot, 8" x 10", with a textured green decoration and gilding on the applied sole and heel. Circa 1950. $35.00.

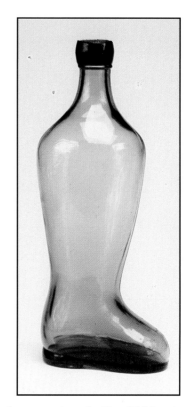

A green boot, 4" x 10½", wine bottle. $5.00 – 10.00.

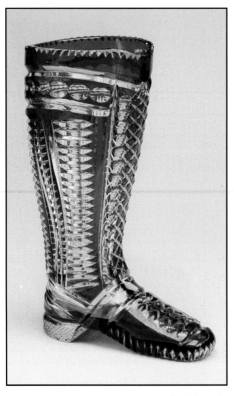

The cranberry cut to crystal boot, 5½" x 7¾". $85.00.

Crystal lady's high shoe bottle, 6" x 11". Marked "Modello – DEPOSITATO." $35.00.

Daisy and Button shoes, 3⅛" x 1¾". **First** — blue Duncan shoe. $20.00. **Second** — blue. $20.00. **Third** — amethyst. $15.00. **Fourth** — cobalt blue. $15.00.

Three boots the dealer referred to as "thirst cups." **Left** – crystal. **Middle** – crystal with a tint applied heel and sole. **Right** – crystal, 2½" x 3½". $15.00 – 20.00 ea.

Tramp or baby shoes, 3" x 2", produced and re-introduced by Boyd Crystal Art Glass, Cambridge, Ohio, are marked with the Boyd logo. **Left** – Bermuda slag, circa 1985. **Right** – deep purple. $15.00 ea.

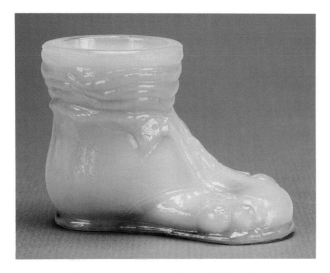

Boyd's Butterscotch. Circa 1979. $15.00.

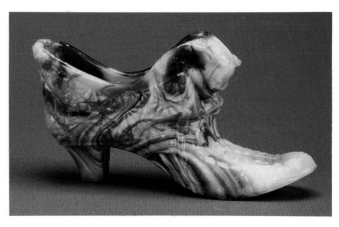

Another reproduction and re-introduction of the cat slipper, 5⅞" x 3", in Bermuda slag. Circa 1985. The mould was one of the Degenhart moulds. $15.00.

Small shoe, 2½", perfume bottle marked "France." $10.00 – 15.00.

Cobalt blue, 2½" x 2¾", Santa boot. Circa 1930. $15.00 – 20.00.

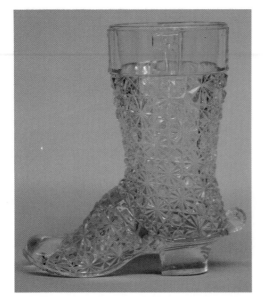

The boot with a spur in crystal, 5¼" x 5½", has the Daisy and Button pattern over the entire boot except for the toe, the top of the boot, and the heel. Circa 1880. Lee plate #203. $125.00 – 145.00.

Green boot, 3⅛" x 4¾", with six buttons on the left side. Circa 1970. $10.00 – 15.00.

Crystal high shoe on skates, same as the middle shoe in the bottom photo on page 86 except it was not made in France. Lee plate #200. $35.00.

Amber, same as the above photo, made in France. $35.00.

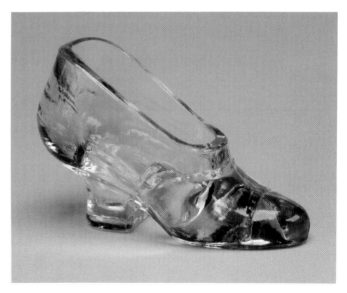

Heavy crystal shoe with a Cuban heel. The beaded band across the vamp, around the shoe, and on the toe is the decoration. Circa 1930. Lee plate #192. $40.00.

Heavy shoes in green and blue, the same as the previous photo. $40.00 ea.

The back of the boot match holder below left.

Aqua boot match holder, 4½" l, with a solid foot, open at the top for matches, striker near the top, and a hole for hanging. Circa 1890. $35.00. They were made in several colors. Beware, these are being reproduced.

Daisy and Button shoes with hollow soles. They were produced in several colors as shown and reproduced and reissued in newer colors than those from the late 1800s. The Depression glass colors are represented along with the newer colors. The appearance of the newer reproduction will be crinkly. $25.00 ea.

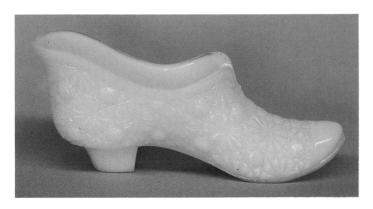

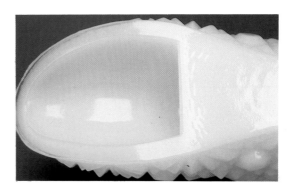

White milk glass Daisy and Button shoe, 4⅞" x 2⅛". Circa 1930. $30.00.

The bottom of the white shoe. Notice the hollow sole.

Gray painted slipper, 4¾" x 2⅝", is simply decorated. Made by Westmoreland Glass Company and marked as such. $15.00.

Same as above.

Blue milk glass Daisy and Button shoe, 5" x 2¼", with sharp, distinct design. Circa 1880. $45.00 – 55.00.

An amber 3¼" x 1½" slipper with a fine mesh on the sole and a solid heel considered hard to find. Lee plate #191. $90.00 – 100.00.

Blue glass, 7¼" x 4½", "Coralene" shoe, open to the toe, with a smooth sole and the marks of the maker. It is decorated with tiny glass beads, which were applied to the enamel paint and heated to set the enamel and fix the beads. Circa 1890. $1,500.00.

The back of the shoe to show the design.

A long, flat high shoe bottle, laced up the front. 3⅓" x 4" long. Circa 1880. Lee plate #182. $75.00.

Crystal thimble holder with white painted flowers. $140.00 – 150.00.

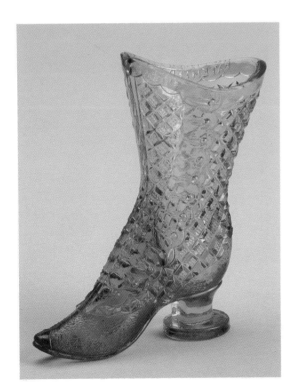

An amber high button shoe in fine cut pattern, 4" x 4½" h, with "PATENTED Dec. 1886" on the top within the scallop. The heel rests on a circle which has "HT" in the center and "Trade Mark" on top and bottom of the circle (holding the shoe with the toe pointing away from you). $100.00 – 125.00.

The bottom of the previous shoe.

A blue boot, 4" x 6½", with enamel decoration around the sole of the toe of the boot and on both sides near the top. Circa 1900. $65.00.

A crystal shoe lamp made by Atterbury and Company, Pittsburgh, PA. 6" x 3½", marked "PATD June 30, 1868." $1,200.00 – 1,500.00.

A spatter boot, 4" x 4", with rigoree encircled around the top and a crystal leaf across the vamp. $110.00 – 135.00.

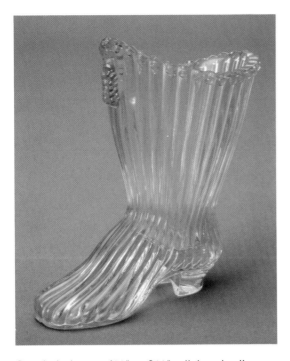

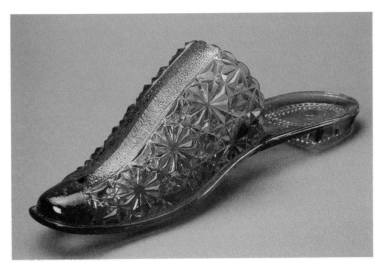

Crystal shoe, 4¼" x 3¼", ribbed all over and has a little tassel hanging down the front. There is a hobnail in each rib or flute around the scalloped top. Lee attributes it to Gillinder & Sons. Lee plate #195. $125.00 – 150.00.

A blue match slipper, 6¼" l, Daisy and Button pattern with a wide panel dividing the design. There is a fine Diamond quilted design over all of the sole. The heel has a hole for hanging. Produced by the United States Glass Co. of Pittsburgh. Circa 1880. Lee plate #192. $120.00 – 150.00.

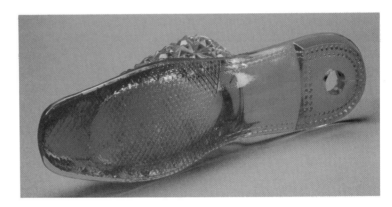

The sole of the match slipper.

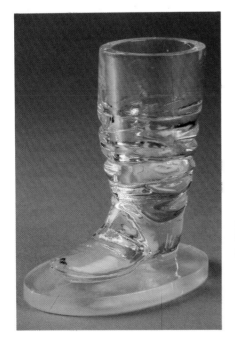

A crystal boot, 3¾", on a satin or frosted oval base, scarce. Circa 1880. Lee plate #184. $100.00.

REPRODUCTIONS AND RE-INTRODUCTIONS

According to the late William Heacock, the difference between a reproduction and a "reintroduction," (terminology he coined) is simple. A reproduction is a copy of an original slipper made much earlier by a factory that no longer exists. A reintroduction is simply taking an old design idea and placing it back on the giftware market in new shapes or in new colors never before made.

Reproductions, when compared to originals, are usually smaller.

Reproductions sold openly and advertised as such should not pose a real threat to the value of older slippers/shoes. There is a scarcity of some glass slippers/shoes and if companies had not made reproductions, many collectors would own very few slippers or shoes, and the variety of colors would not be available.

There is an overall concern because some glass reproductions are so skillfully made that some experienced dealers and collectors can be confused. Reproductions that are crudely made are relatively easy to recognize if one has seen and can recognize well-made shoes.

Klamkin, in *The Collector's Guide to Carnival Glass*, gained praise for the statement that "it is the fear of every collector of American glass that whenever a certain type of glass made in the past becomes collectible, and demand becomes high enough, reproductions are certain to begin appearing on the market." Fakery in glass is rampant because glass can be easily reproduced.

Collectors are grateful to the ethical glass manufacturers whose aim is to produce beautiful glass slippers and have no intention in selling their reproductions to antique dealers to be pawned off as originals. Unfortunately, there are manufacturers whose primary goal is to sell using whatever tactics or means.

Because antique shops are selling antiques and collectibles, reproductions certainly end up there as collectibles without the pretense of being an antique. Reproductions, more often than not, are made in more colors than the originals and in colors that were not used by the older companies. It is because of the improvement in glassmaking in the last 75 years that colors are produced that were perhaps only imagined during the 1800s.

It is sad to report that collectors must be cautious of a few unscrupulous dealers who will knowingly sell a reproduction as an antique to an unwary collector. This blatant abuse will stop when collectors become more knowledgeable and begin asking for written statements about their purchases. The awareness of fraud and fakery enhances the collector's ability to select and buy slippers wisely.

The most disturbing news recently is that glass slippers reproduced in other countries are bought and given to glass repairmen to remove the mark "Made In XXXXX" from the slipper. This flagrant disregard for collectors is one of the primary reasons collectors should be aware and informed. Study, study well-made slippers; the imports can be spotted easily if one looks carefully. I will caution collectors and suggest that they learn to recognize glass for what it is and seek reputable dealers.

Golden amber Daisy and Square shoe on skates, 4¼" x 3⅛" h, by L.E. Smith Co. Circa 1978. A copy of the 1880 shoe skate shown on page 107. $8.00 – 10.00.

The bottom of the shoe skate to show the hollow sole.

Golden amber Daisy and Square shoe skate, 4" l x 2¾" h, circa 1880, has a fine mesh sole. Same as the bottom photo on page 76. $75.00 – 85.00.

The bottom of the shoe to show the mesh sole.

The 6½" l x 5¼" h pink hobnail covered shoe, circa 1984, a reproduction of the Fenton Hobnail covered shoe. The color is not clear, the toe part is wider, and the shoe has a squatty look. "Made in Taiwan" under the toe part on one side. $6.00 – 8.00.

The white milk glass covered shoe, 6½" l x 5¼" h, #3700 MI. A well-made shoe, the hobnails are clear and sharp. Circa 1971. $25.00 – 35.00. Also shown on page 137. This shoe has a tall stately look.

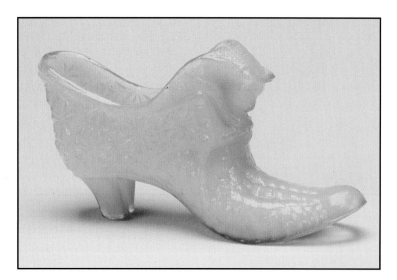

The Crown Tuscan cat slipper, 5⅝" l x 2¾" h, was introduced in the Degenhart line in 1947. The Degenhart slipper can be distinguished from the Columbia cat slipper by the design on the toe part of the shoe and the lack of a protruding lip or edge (around the bottom of the sole and toe area). See Degenhart cat slipper page 126. $60.00.

The toe of the Columbia shoe clearly imitates the look of alligator. Circa 1880. $75.00 – 85.00.

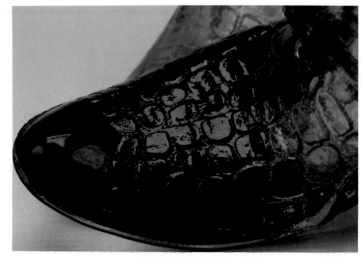

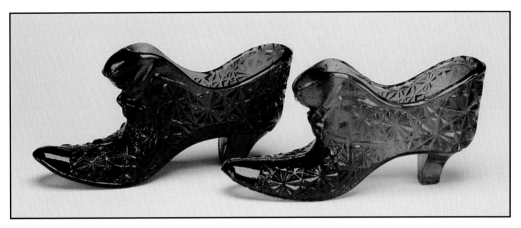

The two Daisy and Button shoes. The quality of the glass and poorly-made shoes make it easy to distinguish them from the well-made Fenton shoes. These are marked "Made in Taiwan." $5.00 – 8.00.

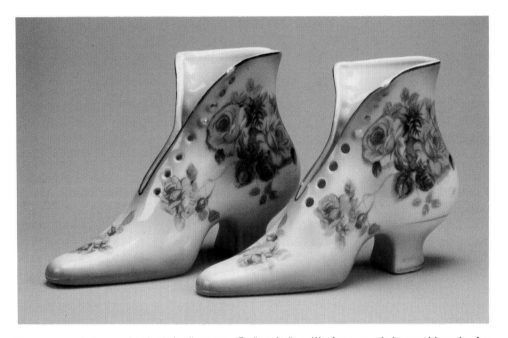

Two porcelain muted pink slippers, 5¼" x 4⅛", with few eyelets and hooks for laces. Circa 1965. $25.00.

The bottom of the slipper. The red wreath with a star and R.S. as a mark is clearly a fake mark, not the mark of Reinhold Schlegelmilch's firm located in the Prussian district of Erfurt, Germany. R.S. Prussia was produced from 1870 through 1950. Collectors must be aware these are being passed off as antiques.

Blue and white brogan, 5¼" x 3¾", same as the bottom of page 39. $35.00 – 45.00.

A copy of the blue and white Old Foley shoe. Slightly larger, thicker, and lacking design on parts of this shoe. Marked "Japan." Circa 1950. $15.00 – 20.00.

DEGENHART GLASS CO.

The Degenhart Crystal Art Glass Company was founded in 1947 by John and Elizabeth Degenhart. In addition to the bells, dishes, owls, and many other small glass objects were the shoes, boots, and slippers made of varying colors and combinations of colors. The production of glass by John Degenhart flourished until his death in 1964.

Mrs. Degenhart continued the operation of the company, employing Zack Boyd until his death in 1968 and later his son Bernard C. Boyd,

who worked part-time. The Degenhart logo was used for the first time in 1972. In 1976, Bernard C. Boyd's full-time job was with Mrs. Degenhart until her death on April 16, 1978, which marked the end of the production of Degenhart glass.

On all of the shoes or boots that are marked, the mark is inside Ⓓ.

The descriptions of the Degenhart slippers and boots were taken from Gene Florence's book, *Degenhart Glass and Paper Weights*, with permission from the Degenhart Museum.

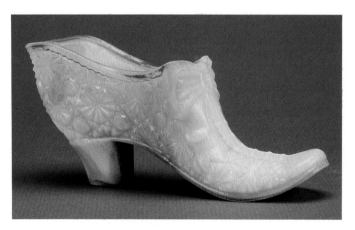

Custard slag colonial bow slipper, without the logo, 5¾" x 2¼", sometimes called Cinderella's slipper, in a Daisy and Button pattern. Introduced in 1947 (mould previously worked at Cambridge Glass Co.). This slipper is currently produced by Raymond Durene Glass Company, formerly the Kanawaha Glass Co. The Degenhart slipper is slightly larger than the Kanawaha-Raymond Durene. The knot of the bow on the Degenhart slipper has three distinct horizontal markings on it. $45.00 – 65.00.

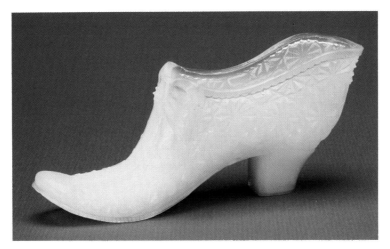

White opalescent slipper, without the logo. Same as the previous photo. $30.00 – 50.00.

Blue, without the logo. Same as the first photo. $30.00 – 50.00.

Left — forest green, **middle** — blue milk, **right** — canary. Same as the first photo, without the logo. $50.00 – 75.00.

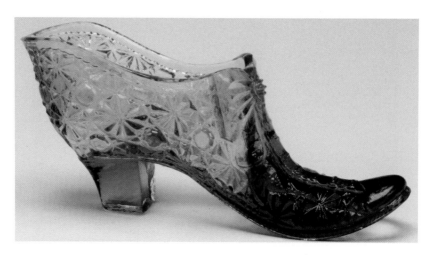

Amber, with logo. Same as the first photo. $45.00 – 60.00.

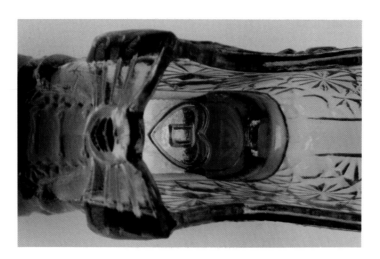

Close-up of the Degenhart logo.

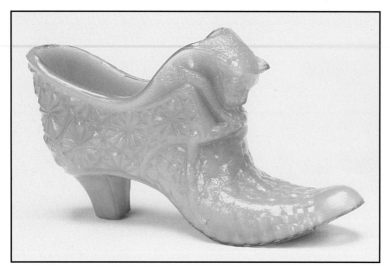

Blue milk glass cat slipper, 5⅝" x 2¾", was introduced in 1947. Reproduction of Columbia Glass of Findlay, Ohio. The Degenhart slipper can be distinguished from the Columbia cat slipper by the lack of a protruding lip or edge, which is found on old slippers around the bottom of the sole (toe area). $30.00 – 50.00.

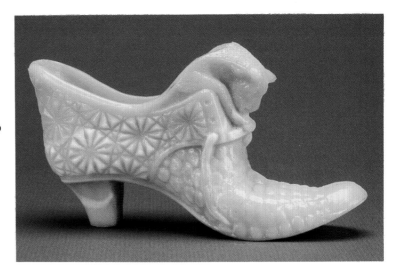

Custard slag, same as the previous photo without the logo. $45.00 – 60.00.

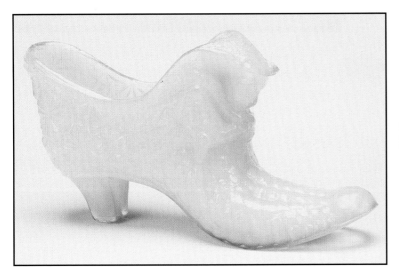

Crown Tuscan, same as above with the logo. $70.00 – 80.00.

White milk glass, same as above without the logo. $30.00 – 50.00.

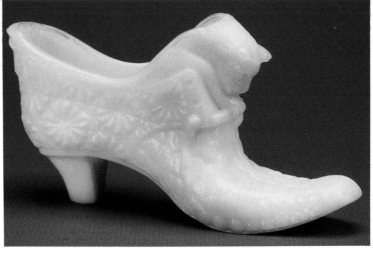

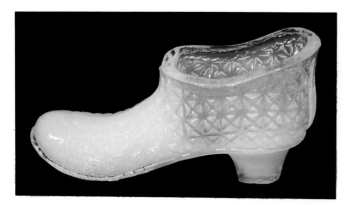

Opalescent miniature slipper, 3⅞" x 1⅞". Introduced in 1965. This is a fine cut with a full sole (with tread marks). Plain around the top opening. Without the logo. $35.00 – 50.00.

Close-up of the bottom of the above slipper.

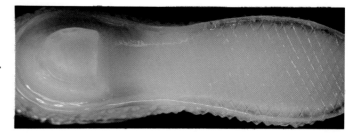

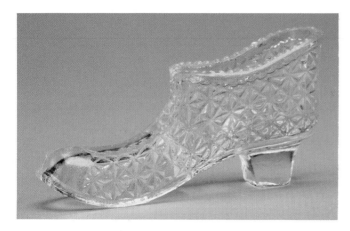

Crystal, 3⅝" x 1⅞", with the modification made in 1966 of the added beaded edge around the top. The sole is hollow. $20.00 – 45.00.

Left — amethyst without logo. $45.00 – 65.00. **Middle** — green with logo. $45.00 – 55.00 **Right** — blue without logo. $45.00 – 65.00. Each one with the 1966 modification of beaded edge and hollow sole.

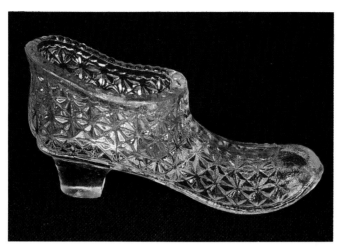

Pink slipper, the same the photo on the top of page 128 except the hollow sole. $45.00 – 65.00.

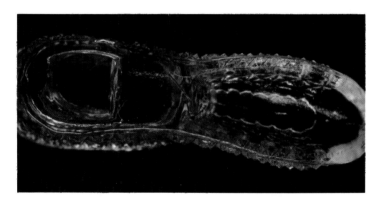

Close-up to show the hollow sole.

Baby shoe toothpick holders, also known as tramp or hobo shoes, 3" x 2⅛", have a definite protruding sole around the shoe. They were introduced and reproduced in 1962 and marked in 1972. The toes are larger, and more of the toes are shown than can be seen on the older ones. **First** — cobalt blue, with the logo. $55.00 – 65.00. **Second** — milk, blue, without the logo. $45.00 – 55.00. **Third** — sapphire, with the logo. $50.00 – 65.00. **Fourth** — Nile green, without the logo. $45.00 – 55.00. **Fifth** — vaseline, without the logo. $45.00 – 55.00.

Cobalt blue Texas boot, 2⅝" x 2⅝", introduced in 1974 and marked in 1974. Mould was made from the Imperial Glass Company mould. $45.00 – 55.00.

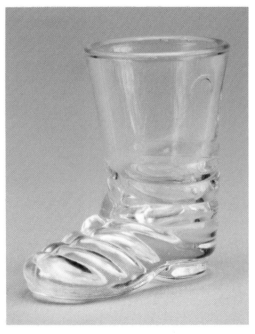

Crystal, same as previous photo. $45.00 – 55.00.

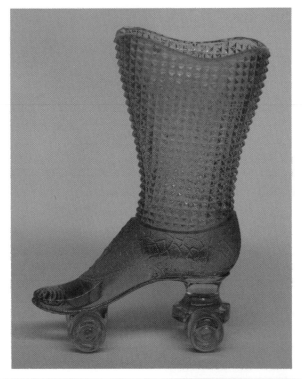

Blue skate boot, 3" x 4⅛", was introduced in 1961. $45.00 – 55.00. Marked in 1974, the reproduction of an 1885 skate boot by Central Glass Works of Wheeling, West Virginia. The Degenhart skate boot was modified around 1967 by adding a beaded edge to the top of the boot. Prior to this date, their boots are found with a plain edge.

The white milk glass bootees, 4⅛" x 2¼", were all made by Lornetta Glass, near Point Marion, Pennsylvania. $50.00 – 60.00. Degenhart was supposed to have made the same bootee. I have seen many of these and cannot distinguish one from the other, were it not for the labels that were affixed to each. According to Gene Florence,

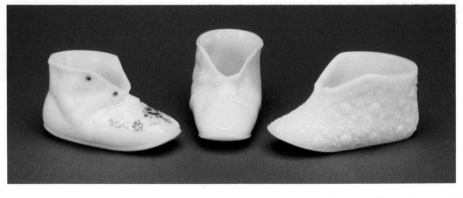

because of the time-consuming procedure, the item was not made very often. Only milk white and custard bootees have been seen, and some are painted with flowers.

130

Custard slag Daisy and Button boot, 4⅝" x 4⅛", was introduced in 1952 and marked in 1972 (this one is not marked). $50.00 – 60.00. This boot is a reproduction of the 1885 George Duncan and Sons of Pittsburgh boot. The Degenhart boots are slightly smaller. The differences can be seen in the glass when comparing Amber Duncan to Amber Degenhart. This boot is also made by Fenton Glass Co., Williamstown, West Virginia. The laces are not as sharp on the Fenton. The scallops are slightly different when comparing. This boot is now being made by the Boyd Crystal Art Glass Company, Cambridge, Ohio.

Amber Daisy and Button boot, the same the top of page 130. $50.00 – 65.00.

Close-up to show the laces.

MOSSER GLASS CO.

Mosser Glass factory has an interesting history, starting with Thomas (Tom) R. Mosser, who began working for Cambridge Glass Company as a teenager, where he learned the glass-making trade and an appreciation for beautiful handmade glass objects. The Cambridge Glass Company closed in 1954. Tom dreamed of having his own glass company, and in 1959, with his skills, made the dream come true and began glass production. He purchased the present property at Route 22 East in 1971, where three of his four children were employed.

He continues to enjoy success for authentic reproductions of early American glassware, which allows shoe collectors to select several styles of well-made slippers and boots in beautiful colors from moulds made during the early 1900s, and others designed by Mosser.

According to Tom Mosser, "The glassware enjoyed today will be tomorrow's cherished pieces." There is pride which is displayed in the little slippers and boots as well as other pieces of decorative and utilitarian glass.

Slippers with bows, 4½" x 2¼", solid sole and heel, Mosser #109, introduced in 1973. From **left** to **right** – cobalt blue, ice blue, pink, amethyst, red, green, and amber. $15.00 – 20.00 each.

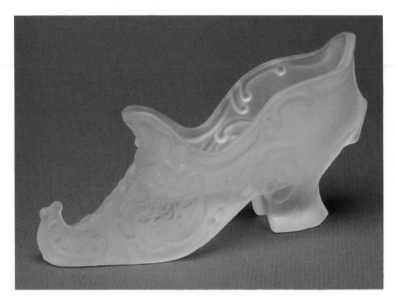

Frosted slipper, 5¾" x 3", introduced in 1973, listed as "Rose slipper #117" in the Mosser line. It is currently produced in several of the Mosser colors. $25.00 – 30.00.

These fine cut boots, 4⅜" x 4¼", have a hollow toe and solid heel. They were introduced in 1973 and are currently being produced in several colors. From **left** to **right** — amethyst, green, and pink satin finish. $15.00 – 25.00.

Close-up to show the pattern.

Yellow, same as above.

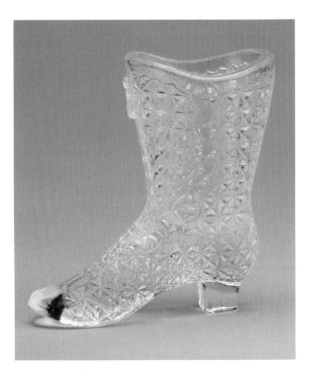

Crystal, same as above.

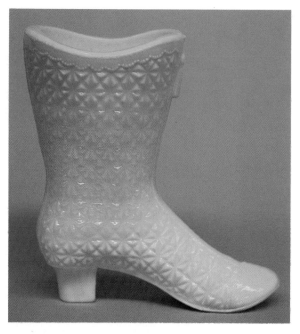

Opalescent milk glass, same as previous photo.

This boot, 3⅞" x 3⅛", as introduced in the Mosser line in 1975. It has a spur and indentation on the sole. Marked with the Mosser logo. $15.00 – 25.00.

Close-up to show indentation on the sole.

Same as above.

FENTON GLASS CO.

Fenton handmade glass went into production in 1907 in Williamstown, West Virginia. Various designs of paper labels have been used since the 1900s. Fenton produced slippers under the name "Olde Virginia Glass" for approximately five years prior to 1973. The slippers are marked "OVG" on the bottom. The "Olde Virginia Glass" line was sold to stores which did not sell the regular Fenton line. In 1970, Fenton re-introduced carnival glass and began to mark all their items with the embossed "Fenton" in an oval on the bottom.

Slippers, boots, and shoes were produced in various colors and patterns. Two different kitten slippers, one in the hobnail and the other in Daisy and Button were produced.

The hobnail slipper is made by blowing or pressing the glass into a mould. Each hobnail shows in the mould as a deep dimple, which becomes the raised part of the finished slipper. The slippers with the opalescence demand skillful cooling and rewarming to bring out the opacity of the edge and hobs in the opalescent hobnail slipper. Each slipper is 5⅛" x 3".

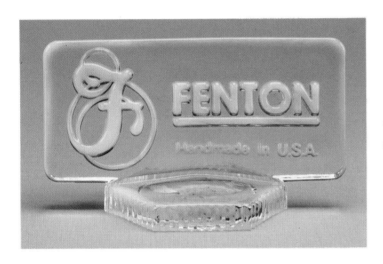

The Fenton logo in opalescent glass. $30.00 – 35.00.

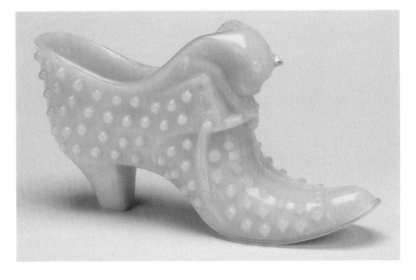

Green pastel, #3995 GP. No logo, circa 1950, has a magenta and silver label. $35.00 – 50.00.

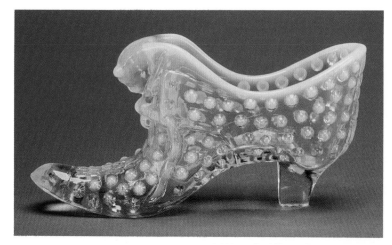

Topaz opalescent, #3995 TO. No logo, circa 1939 – 1944. Disc. 1948. Re-issued 1962. $35.00 – 50.00.

Milk glass, #3995 MI. No logo, circa 1950, has a magenta and silver label. $35.00 – 45.00.

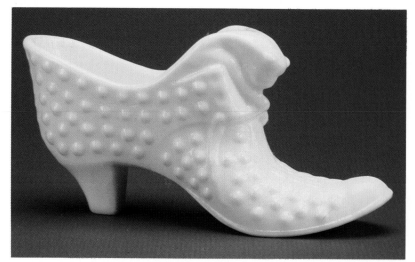

Left — ruby, #3995 RU, circa 1996. No logo or label. $35.00 – 45.00. **Middle** — orange, #3995 OR, circa 1964. No logo. $35.00 – 45.00. **Right** — colonial amber, #3995 CA, circa 1962. $35.00 – 45.00.

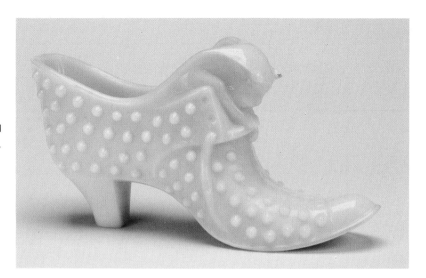

Rose pastel, #3995 RP, no logo. Circa 1954, has a magenta and silver label. $35.00 – 50.00.

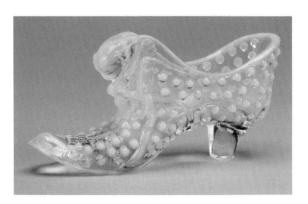

French opalescent, #3995 FO. No logo. Circa 1939, discontinued 1950. $35.00 – 50.00.

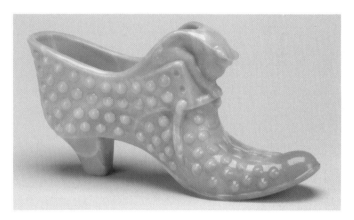

Blue pastel, #3995 BP, no logo. Circa 1954, discontinued 1955. $35.00 – 50.00.

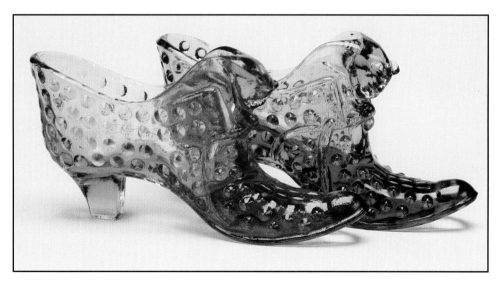

Left — clear green, #3995 CG. No logo. Circa 1961, discontinued 1962. $35.00 – 45.00. **Right** — colonial green, #3995 CG. Circa 1963. $30.00 – 40.00.

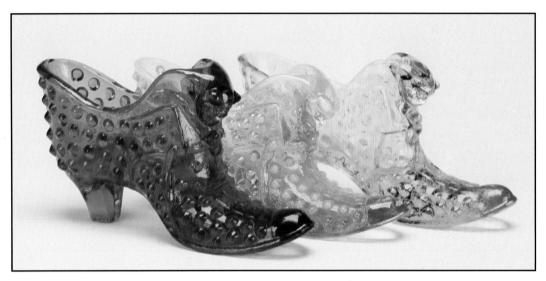

Left — colonial blue, #3995 CB. No logo. Circa 1964. $35.00 – 45.00. **Middle** — blue opalescent, #3995 BO. Circa 1930, discontinued 1950. Was made again 1953 through 1955. Last made 1960 through 1964. $45.00 – 55.00. **Right** — amber, #3995 A. No logo. Circa 1964. $35.00 – 45.00.

White covered hobnail shoe, #3700 MI, 6½" x 5¼". Circa 1971 for a short time, with logo. $55.00 – 65.00.

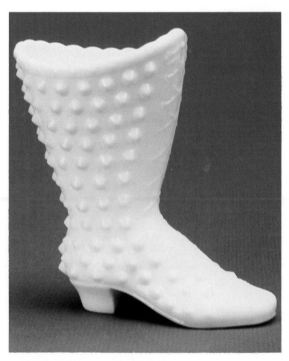

Milk white hobnail boot, #3992 MI. Circa 1971 with logo. $20.00 – 30.00.

Pink hobnail boot, same as previous photo. $20.00 – 30.00.

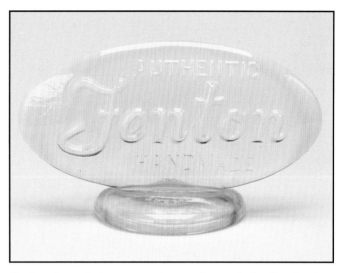

Fenton logo in topaz opalescent, made for the Fenton Glass Collector's Association, 1980. $30.00 – 40.00.

The Daisy and Button slipper as well as the boot has continued to be popular, evidenced by the continuation of the pattern.

Left — boot, #1990, shading from yellow to orange, with logo. $25.00 – 30.00. **Middle** — colonial green, #1990, no logo. $25.00 – 30.00. **Right** — boot in canary, #1990. No logo. $30.00 – 40.00.

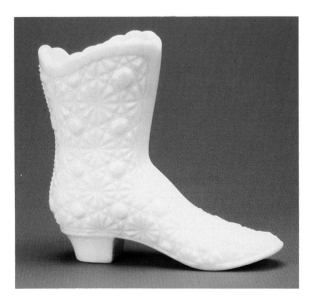

White milk glass, #1990 MI, no logo. $30.00 – 40.00.

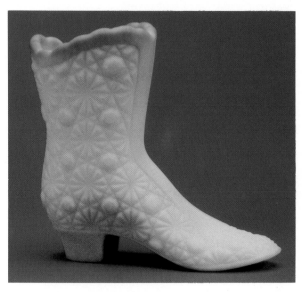

Burmese, #1990 BR, with logo. Circa 1986. $25.00 – 30.00.

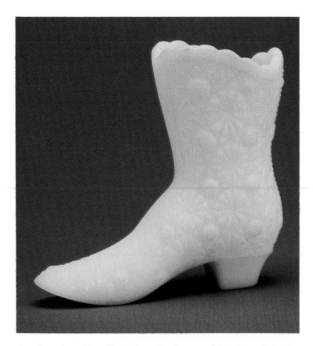

Custard satin, #1990, with logo. $25.00 – 30.00.

Left — amethyst with iridescence, #1990 (carnival), re-introduced in 1971 with logo. $35.00 – 45.00.
Right — amber, #1990, no logo. $40.00 – 50.00.

Vaseline slipper, #1995 V, no logo. Circa 1939. $40.00 – 50.00.

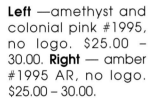

Left — dense white slipper, #1995 MI. $25.00 – 30.00. Right — pale opaque custard, #1993 OC, circa 1971. $25.00 – 30.00.

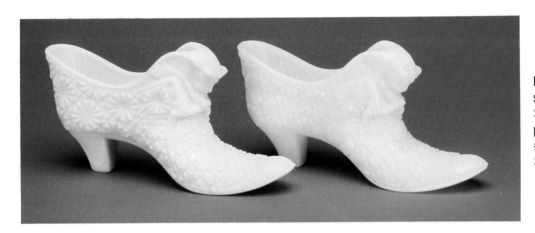

Left —amethyst and colonial pink #1995, no logo. $25.00 – 30.00. Right — amber #1995 AR, no logo. $25.00 – 30.00.

The rose slipper, 6" x 3", introduced 1-1-1990, was designed by Tony Rosena, a Fenton regular designer. Left — pink, Middle — dusty rose, Right — black (dark amethyst). $25.00 each.

Left – colonial blue, #1995 CB, no logo, circa 1964. $30.00 – 40.00. **Middle** – federal blue, #1995 with logo. $25.00 – 30.00. **Right** – aqua, #1995 with logo. $25.00 – 30.00.

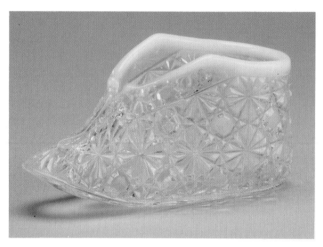

French opalescent bootee, #1994 FO. No logo. $35.00 – 50.00.

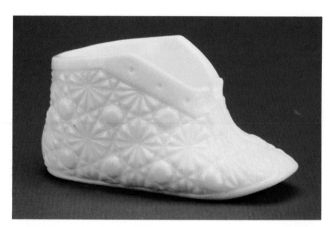

White bootee, #1994 M. No logo. These bootees and slippers were produced in several colors. $25.00 – 30.00.

Satin custard shoe, 4¾" x 2½", made from an old design and hand painted with pink flowers. No logo, has a paper label inside and underneath, hand painted and signed by the artist. $30.00 – 35.00.

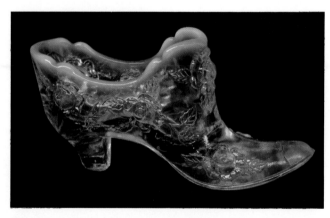

Green with opalescent edge, #1995, no logo. $40.00 – 50.00.

METAL SHOES

IDENTIFICATION

To identify and date American sterling silver, one must rely on the scholarly research of writers. America did not have an established guild or hall for keeping records as England had. American sterling is identified by the maker's marks (their initials) and/or trademarks of the manufacturer. (The word sterling silver came into use in the United States after 1860 and guarantees that the silver is ".925 pure or fine.")

In England, craftsman's guild rules required silversmiths to stamp their wares with hallmarks that indicated the maker, his town, the year, the reigning monarch, and the mark that certifies that the object meets the standard of quality. (England does not use the word sterling.)

Several silver companies in America produced slippers and shoes. Two companies in particular appear to have produced larger quantities and therefore will have a little background information mentioned.

Gorham Silver Company, founded in 1831 in Providence, Rhode Island, registered their trademark, #33902, which is the lion, anchor, and Gothic G in the early 1860s, according to the information provided by Mr. Samuel J. Hough of Brown University.

The B2124 pincushion in the shape of a small shoe was first made in May 1903, and was stamped out in batches of 100. A batch could be made for $113.48, with 25 hours spent on applying the cushions, 15 minutes per piece.

Gorham produced a larger pincushion, B3189, in February 1907. It weighed 9 oz. 4 dwt. (valued at $7.36) and required 5½ hours of a silversmith's time to make at a cost of $1.93. Stamping required 50 minutes (cost 33 cents), piercing (all those holes) took an astounding 11¾ hours (labor cost $3.52), and engraving was an hour (cost 33 cents).

The disparity between the cost of the two slipper pincushions led Mr. Hough to consult a designer at Gorham to be sure that the B3189 cost record did not also represent a batch. He was assured that those figures represent the actual cost of making a single pincushion.

It was discovered by the early metal designers and silversmiths that anything that could be made from silver could be made from other metals. Once a mould for metal shoes was made, the style was rarely changed, due to the expense of designing and making the mould. A mould could be used to produce hundreds of shoes that were used as souvenirs for various cities or events.

In 1888, Mr. Edward Austin Jennings of Bridgeport, Connecticut, founded the American Jewelry Company with his brother, Erwin Jennings. A few years later the brothers reorganized the company, calling it the Jennings Brothers Manufacturing Company, producing silverware art metals and reproductions of Sheffield plate. The trademark of Jennings Brothers is J.B., with four numbers; This was used through the late 1940s. Jennings Brothers produced novelty slippers and shoes of pewter or Britannia and plated them with silver or copper.

Pewter is an alloy of tin and copper or an alloy of the low melting point metals, including lead, bismuth, and antimony. The higher the tin content, the better the pewter. Pewter shoes are duller, darker, and softer than silver. Pewter melts if placed directly over heat, and it also corrodes and develops tiny potmarks.

Some slippers made of Britannia resemble pewter so closely that sometimes it is mistaken for pewter. Britannia has the same metals as pewter, but with more antimony and copper. This metal is brighter in appearance (not as bright as silver), does not bend as easily as pewter, and is more durable.

Gorham; Small wares catalog 1910 – 1911.

THE OWL AT THE BRIDGE
SAMUEL J. HOUGH • 25 BERWICK LANE
CRANSTON, R.I. 02905-3708 • (401) 467-7362

Report on Gorham Silver Pincushion B3189

The B3189 Pincushion was an unusually large novelty. First made 16 February 1907, it weighed 9 oz. 4 dwt. (valued at $7.36) and required 5 1/2 hours of silversmith's time to make, at a cost of $1.93. Stamping required 50 minutes (cost, 33 cents); piercing (all those holes) took an astounding 11 3/4 hours (labor cost $3.52); and engraving was an hour (cost, 33 cents).

The red velvet cost 35 cents and required 3 hours to insert (cost, 90 cents). Stoning of 25 minutes (cost, 8 cents); bobbing of 1 3/4 hours (44 cents); and finishing of 3/4 hour (cost 23 cents) brought the sum of silver, materials, and labor to $15.47, to which was added 20% overhead ($3.06), 40% profit ($6.18), and $1.24 for administrative costs, for a net factory price of $25.98 which was rounded to $30.

This contrasts with the B2124 Pincushion in the shape of a small shoe. These were first made in May 1903 and were stamped out in batches of 100. A batch could be made for $113.48, with 25 hours spent on applying the cushions, 15 minutes per piece.

The disparity between the cost of the two led me to consult a designer at Gorham to be sure that the B3189 cost record didn't also represent a batch. I was assured that those figures represent the actual cost of making a single Pincushion.

Samuel J. Hough

A silver pin cushion, 2", in repoussé (a raised decoration in an overall pattern). Circa 1860. Early English mark on the bottom. $225.00.

Close-up of above.

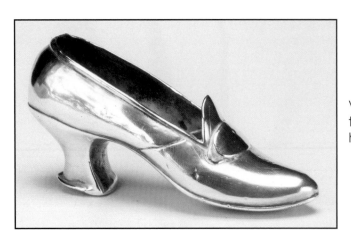

Victorian sterling slipper, 3½" x 1¾". Circa 1903, with the Gorham mark and numbers B2124 under the heel. $175.00 – 200.00.

Sterling Victorian pin cushion, 2¾" x¾", highly decorated except for the plain toe and heel. Circa 1890. $200.00.

Sterling pin cushion, 3½" x 1¾". Three tiny buttons close the chased straps. Circa 1874. $300.00.

Two sterling slipper pincushions, 3½" x 1¾". **Left** — green cushion. **Right** — a burgundy cushion. Both circa 1903, have the Gorham mark, and number B2124 under the heels. $175.00 – 200.00 ea.

A pair of sterling "Geta" salt and pepper shakers, 3" x ⅛". Circa 1930. $200.00 – 250.00.

Sterling high shoe with spat pincushion, 3" x 2¼", with three buttons on the side. Circa 1910. $175.00.

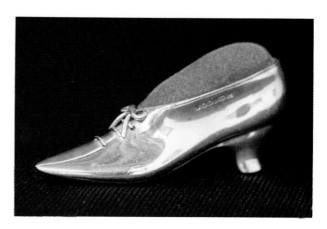

Silver 2¼" pincushion neatly laced. British marks. Circa 1852. $175.00 – 200.00.

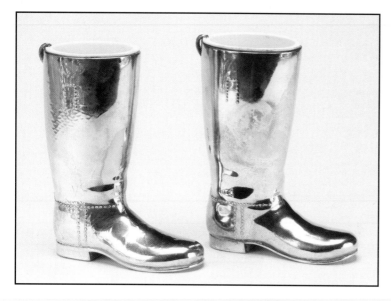

Silver-plate riding boots, 4" x 2½", designed to hold liquid. **Left** — boot has a measurement "approx 1½ oz." on the sole. **Right** — boot has a measurement "approx 1¾ oz." on the sole. Made in England. $50.00 – 75.00 ea.

Left — small silver-plate boot with a spur, 1½" x 1¾". Circa 1950. $30.00. **Right** — sterling silver slipper with an engraved and chased dragon design. Circa 1900. $65.00.

Silver-plate high-heeled pincushion, 3" x 3", with a maroon velvet cushion. Circa 1950. $35.00 – 45.00.

Large silver-plate pincushion, 6½" x 3¾". The pointed toe has decoration over the front, around the entire shoe, and on the buttoned strap. Circa 1930. Marked J.B. 1026. $60.00 – 75.00.

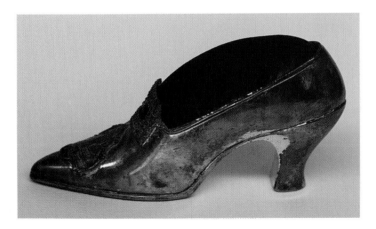

Large silver-plate pincushion, 6" x 3", has a buckle, the crest on the toe has a relief design of Los Angeles, Calif. City Hall. Circa 1930, marked J.B. 1904. $70.00 – 85.00.

Silver-plate boot pincushion, 3" x 2¼", with brown cushion. Marked J.B., circa 1950. This boot was also made in sterling silver. $65.00 – 75.00.

Large silver-plate pincushion, 6" x 3", with a crest of the Statue of Liberty. Marked J.B. 1104. $65.00 – 75.00.

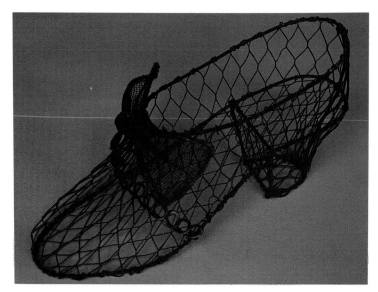

8" x 4" wire slipper complete with bow. Circa 1991. $20.00.

Four pincushions. **First** — a bronze metal, 3" x 2½", has a flat bow. Circa 1920. $35.00 – 45.00. **Second** — pewter 2¾" x 2½" shoe with green laces. Circa 1920, marked "England." $65.00 – 75.00. **Third** — 2¾" x 2½", has a crest of the Empire State Building on the vamp. Circa 1920. **Fourth** — pewter, 3" x 2½", with openings for laces. Circa 1920, marked "Britannia." $35.00 – 45.00.

Heavy silver-colored metal men's shoe, 4¾" x 2". The tongue of the shoe designed to hold a cigarette. It has eyelets and hooks for strings. Circa 1950. On the side of the heel is the wording "Peltro Italy." $45.00.

More pincushions. **First** — 3¾" x 2" with maroon cushion and the Capital building on the crest of the vamp. Circa 1920. $35.00 – 45.00. **Second** — copper, 3¼" x 1¾", with a red cushion and a bow at the top. Circa 1920. $25.00 – 35.00. **Third** — same as the bottom photo on page 146. $200.00. **Fourth** — same as the top photo on page 146. $225.00.

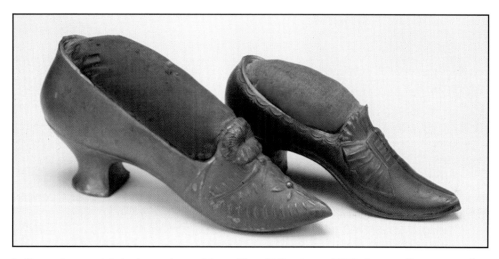

Left — Large Victorian pincushion, 7" x 3¾", circa 1909, has a flower on the vamp. $100.00. **Right** — brown metal pincushion with red cushion, 4¼" x 2", circa 1920. $40.00 – 45.00.

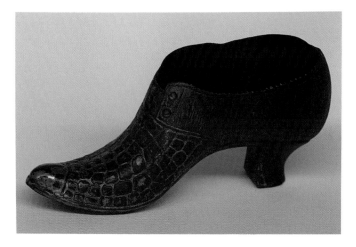

Silver-plate pincushion, 5½" x 2¾". The front of the shoe has an alligator pattern and openings for laces. Circa 1920. $45.00 – 55.00.

Left — pewter 3¾" x 2" pincushion with green laces. Circa 1920. $45.00. **Right** — pewter pincushion, 3¾" x 2", with red velvet cushion and open eyelets. Both bought in England. $45.00.

Heavy brass pincushion with silverplating, 5½" x 3", in the Daisy and Button pattern, has openings for laces. Circa 1920. $40.00.

Pincushion, 4" x 1", with traces of silver-plate, has a bow on the vamp. Circa 1900. (This pincushion was also made in sterling silver.) $85.00.

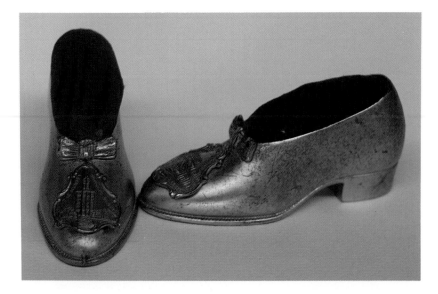

Two gold painted pincushions, 4¼" x 2¼". The **left** has a crest of Union Station, Chicago. Marked "J.B. 1852". $35.00 – 45.00. **Right** has a crest of the Wrigley Building, Chicago. Marked "J.B. 1852." Circa 1920. $45.00.

Shoe skate pincushion, 2¾" x 1¾". Circa 1896. (The skates actually roll.) $75.00.

Pincushion, 4" x 3", with a bow on the vamp. Marked "USA" on the bottom. Circa 1920. $40.00 – 50.00.

Pincushion, 3½" x 2", has traces of silverplate and a crest on the vamp depicting the symbols of the Trylon and Perisphere of the New York World's Fair, 1939. $75.00.

Copper pincushion, 2½" x 1", has flowers decorating the sides of the slipper. Circa 1920. $50.00.

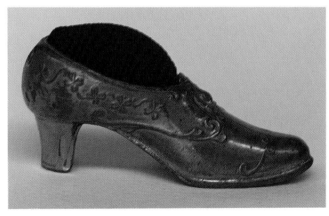

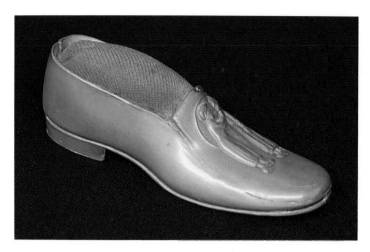

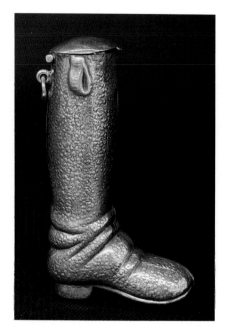

Copper-plated pincushion, 4½" x 1¼", with red cushion, two ladies listed as "gossipers." Circa 1920. $30.00 – 45.00.

A sterling 2½" boot that held needles. This boot was attached to a chatelaine. Circa 1860. $65.00.

Victorian 7" x 3⅜" pewter slipper with copper plating, circa 1900. This slipper was produced in silver plate. On the sole, "200th Performance of Henry W. Savage's musical success *The Merry Widow*, Colonial Theater, Chicago, April 29, 1909." J.B. Trademark. $125.00 – 150.00.

The sole of the previous shoe.

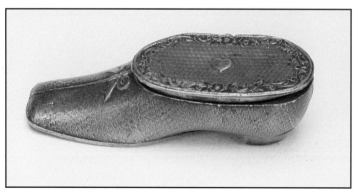

Victorian snuff box in the shape of a shoe, 2½" x 1½", has a hinged lid that has a tiny heart decorating the top of the lid. Circa 1876. $200.00 – 225.00.

Three different shoes. **Left** — gray metal, 2½" x 2", with laces, an open shoe with treading on the sole. Circa 1910. $20.00. **Middle** — men's brogan has the tongue hanging down and a hole in the sole. Circa 1930. $45.00. **Right** — gray men's shoe, 2¼" x 1". Circa 1930. On the sole, "made in Japan #444." $35.00.

Pewter slipper, 4" x 1", with a bow on the vamp, with traces of silver-plate. On the sole "Souvenir – World's Exposition Chicago, 1893." $100.00 – 125.00.

Close-up of the previous slipper.

Copper 5" x 4½" ink well. Circa 1920. $45.00 – 65.00.

Heavy brass slipper, 4" x 2½", decorated with swirls of brass and a frog on the vamp. Circa 1920, marked "England." $45.00.

Pewter ice cream mould, #570, 6" x 3½". Circa 1918. $50.00. By the mid-1900s, ice cream moulds were difficult to find. I recently read that the oldest and largest ice cream mould manufacturers in this country were Eppelsheimer & Co. of New York, whose moulds were marked "E&Co."; and Schall & Co., also of New York, with "S&Co." The moulds that are marked with raised relief numbers indicate size. Because pewter is soft, some of the manufacturers marks and/or numbers have blurred or rubbed off completely due to constant handling.

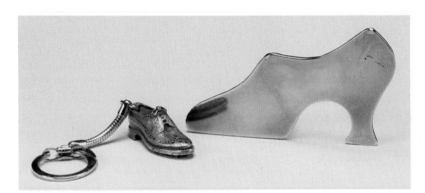

Left — a salesman's sample of "Walkover" shoes for men. $20.00 – 30.00. **Right** — brass 7" x 3" ladies' shoe sample. Circa 1920. $30.00 – 45.00.

Left — copper-plated slipper, 3½" x 1¾", with a bow on the vamp. Circa 1920. $35.00. **Middle** — copper-plated 3" x 1¾" slipper with the Capitol building on the crest. $25.00. **Right** — copper slipper, 2½" x 1". Flowers decorate the sides of the slipper. Circa 1920. $45.00.

Brass slipper, 3¾" x ¾", with blue stones around the entire slipper. Inside, the word "TURKEY." Circa 1950. $50.00.

Two heavy brass shoes, 2⅞" x 1¾", with mice on the top and sides of the shoes. The shoe on the left has the wording "Ye Lucky Lyme Regis Boot," on the sole "Made in England." Circa 1950. $25.00.

Brass high shoe, 4¼" x 5½", laced in front. Circa 1990. Marked India. $10.00.

Pewter "Old Woman Who Lived in a Shoe" 1¼" x 1½", with three people, two are ½" and one is ¼". Circa 1965. $15.00.

Black iron high shoe on a tray, circa 1950, marked "Wilton." $10.00.

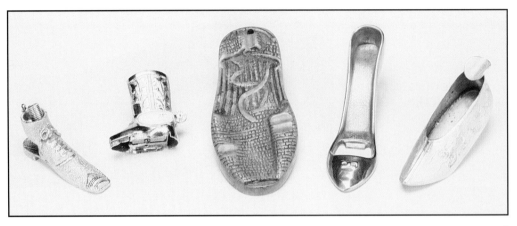

An assortment of metal shoes. **First** — a 3" x1¾" gray metal paper and pencil holder. $5.00. **Second** — a 2" x 2" yellow metal cowboy boot, pencil sharpener, "Souvenir of Las Vegas." $5.00. **Third** — a brass sandal, 5⅛" x ¼", complete with laces is an ashtray. $5.00. **Fourth** — a brass slipper, 5" x 1¾", bottle opener. $8.00. **Fifth** — a sterling, chased and engraved slipper, 4" x ¾" decorated with dragons on both sides, a coin forms the holder for a cigarette. $50.00 – 65.00.

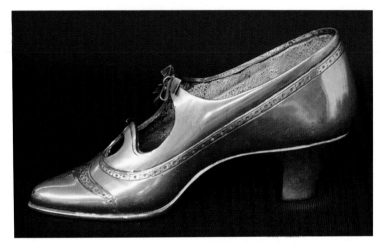

Large silver-plate shoe, 6½" x 3¾", the same as the top left photo on page 149 except for the bow and minus the cushion. $45.00.

Shoe with a pencil attached, 2". Circa 1930, Japan. $25.00.

Black painted slipper ashtray, 6½" x 1", decorated with silver inlay. Circa 1936. $20.00.

MISCELLANEOUS SHOES

Two celluloid slipper knives, 2" x ¾". On the knife blade is "Lenox Cutlery-New York." Circa 1910. $60.00 – 75.00.

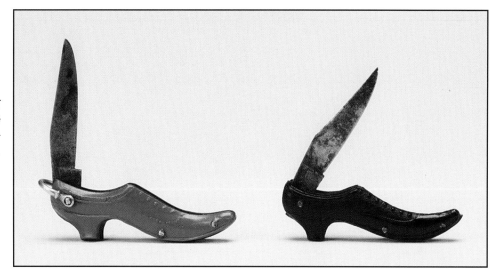

A 1" slipper pipe , $10.00, and a moccasin pipe holder, 6" x 1½". Circa 1920. $20.00 – 25.00.

A shoe pipe marked "Bruyere Garantie Lovueni Canada." Circa 1950. $35.00 – 50.00.

Two men's shoes that were used in advertising. **Left —** burgundy colored suede shoe, 4½" x 1¼". On the sole, "Relax in Slax." Circa 1950. $25.00 – 35.00. **Right —** burgundy colored plastic shoe, 2½" x 1". On the sole, "Nunn Bush." Circa 1955. $30.00 – 40.00.

A decanter with six boots, each one is 2" x 2". Circa 1939. "Made in Japan" on the bottom of the decanter. $35.00.

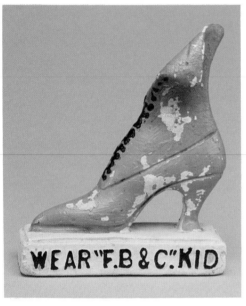

Chalkware shoe used for advertising. Circa 1900. Bought in Gallipolis, Ohio. $65.00.

A shoe telephone that really works. Circa 1980. $30.00.

Left — a hand-carved and painted kitten in a shoe to hang on a Christmas tree. Circa 1970. $20.00. **Right** — plastic white bear in a shoe. Marked "Made in Occupied Japan." $15.00.

A pair of leather shoes from Europe. The note attached indicated they were worn in 1873 by a young child. $125.00.

A hanging pin cushion. $65.00.

A wooden carved shoe with distinct details including holes for laces. $50.00.

Tan shoe, 3" x 2", with a western scene around the entire shoe. On the side, the word "Arbro." This shoe resembles ivory or bone. Circa 1930. $35.00.

Left — blue and white ashtray, 4" x 2½", Dutch style slipper. $25.00. **Right** — blue and white 3" x ¾" lighter. $40.00.

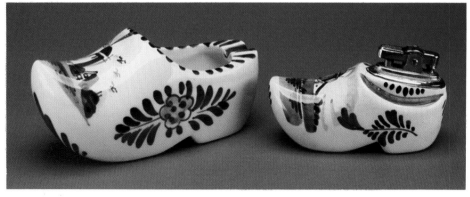

Shoes decorated with blue and white. **Left** — a sterling silver spoon with a blue and white miniature shoe ½", circa 1959. $10.00 – 15.00. **Middle** — a shoe pin, 2", circa 1972. $6.00. **Right** — a pair of wooden slippers, 2⅝" x 1⅜", circa 1972, hand painted. Marked "Holland." $10.00 – 15.00.

An assortment of miniature leather shoes, $15.00 each; earrings, etc. measuring ⅛" to 1". $10.00 each.

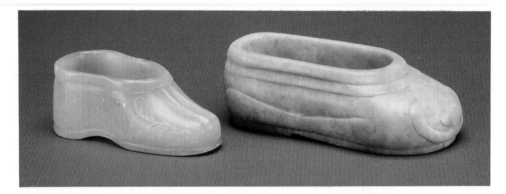

Soapstone shoes from China. **Left** — 3" x 2" carved shoe. $20.00 – 30.00. **Right** — 4" x 2", slightly heavier than the one on the left and carved with more detail. Circa 1930. $35.00 – 50.00.

FIGURAL SHOES

Slippers and shoes have not lost their popularity, as evidenced by Avon and other companies.

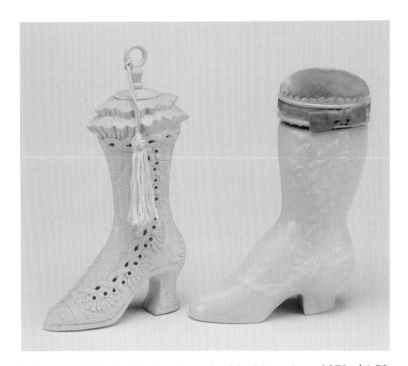

Left — a pink plastic boot sachet holder, circa 1978. $4.50.
Right — blue glass boot pin cushion, circa 1972. $5.00 – 6.00.

Left — high buttoned glass shoe, circa 1970. **Middle** — shoe skate, circa 1980. **Right** — glass boot, maker unknown. $3.00 – 4.00 each.

Left — petite glass slipper perfume bottle, circa 1973. $4.00 – 5.00. **Right** — pink soap slipper with glass bow-shaped perfume bottle, circa 1970. $6.00 – 8.00.

Left — brown glass cowboy boot, circa 1965. $4.00 – 5.00. **Right** — brown glass riding boot with metal strap on the top, circa 1966. $4.00 – 5.00.

Frilly plastic boot, circa 1978. $3.50 – 4.00.

A golden slipper was awarded to one winning district of each branch in Avon's 73rd Anniversary contest. Originally, a 1 oz. topaz was inside the slipper. $25.00 ($125.00 if complete).

Left — green glass boot with red top in the Christmas specials, circa 1967. $3.00. **Right** — green glass boot once held Faberge Brut for men, eau de cologne. $3.50 – 4.00.

SHOES FROM JAPAN

The collecting of shoes or items marked "Made in Occupied Japan" allows one to collect historical items.

Prior to the United States' occupation of Japan, items were marked "Japan" and "Made in Japan." During the occupation in 1945 until the end of the occupation on April 28, 1952, all items exported to the United States had to be marked "Made in Occupied Japan." The colors used for marking "Japan," "Made in Japan," and "Occupied Japan" were black, red, or green with green being the hardest to find. The color used does not add to or detract from the value of the shoe. As with any shoe from any country, collect what you like and buy the best you can.

An "Occupied Japan" ceramic 6" x 2" h slipper, painted with blue flowers, tan and green leaves. $15.00 – 25.00.

A blue 4" x 3¼" ceramic shoe with Jiminy Cricket sitting across the vamp. $20.00 – 25.00.

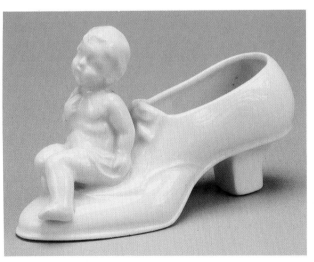

A black ceramic high-heeled slipper, 9" x 5½", trimmed with silver (used as part of a store display for jewelry). $20.00.

A white ceramic slipper, 4¾" x 2½", with a cherub on the vamp. $25.00.

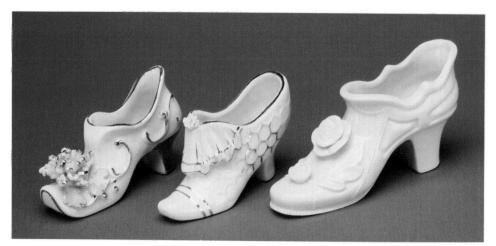

Three ceramic slippers. **Left** — 3" x 2", decorated with a pink flower on the toe and a gold heel. $20.00. **Middle** — 3" x 2", trimmed with gold tassel on the vamp. **Right** — white, 5" x 3", with white flowers on the vamp and toe. $25.00.

Three stylish ceramic slippers. **Left** — a wall hanger in the shape of a high-heeled sandal, 5½" x 3", decorated with hand-painted flowers, bow, and applied flowers on the toe. $20.00. **Middle** — white, 4½" x 3", with pale blue, high-heeled 40-ish style. $15.00. **Right** — high-heeled, 3½" x 4", with a net flower on the toe. $20.00.

A porcelain mule-type slipper, 3" x 2", with blue and rust hand-painted designs over entire slipper and inside of the heel. $20.00.

High-heeled 4" x 3" blue ceramic shoe copied from a glass shoe of the 1940s. $40.00.

Three white ceramic shoes. **Left** — 2" x 1¾", with openings for laces, trimmed with a silver bow on the vamp. $15.00. **Middle** — 3½" x 2", with a white bow and openings for strings. $25.00. **Right** — 2¼" x 1½", with pink and blue flowers and gilding around the upper shoe. $20.00.

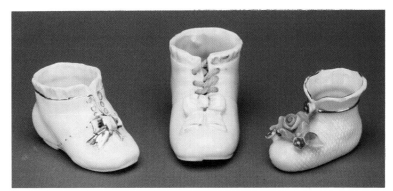

Left — 2½" x 1¾", white irridized with a blue flower on the vamp. $15.00. **Middle** — white Dutch style 4¼" x 2" slipper with a red flower and green leaves. $10.00. **Right** — white slipper, 4" x 2½", with a red flower on the vamp. $10.00.

Left — teal blue slipper, 4" x 2½", has a bow on the vamp, a ruffle, and flower around the top. "Made in Occupied Japan." $15.00. **Right** — 3" x 2", blue slipper decorated with a teal blue bow. $20.00.

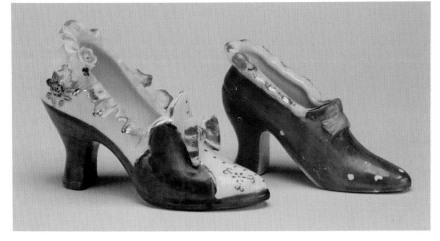

Left — a white slipper, 5" x 2½", with a flat bow across the vamp with gilding as decoration. $25.00 **Right** — white porcelain slipper, 7" x 2", decorated with hand-painted roses and gilding, "3764" on the side of the heel. $20.00.

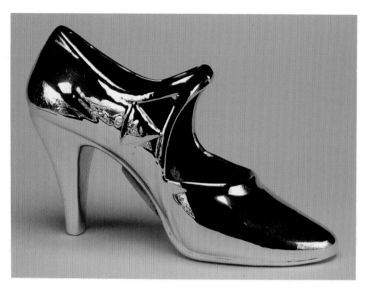

A 6½" x 7" high-heeled slipper held by a pair of hands, decorated with pink roses and gilded lace. Circa 1960. $45.00.

Silver slipper, 9" x 5½", with a bow across the instep. Underneath on a paper label, "Exclusively for Lina Lee – Beverly Hills - New York." $20.00.

Left — hand-painted slipper, 4" x 2½", with a pink applied rose across the front near the toe and hand-painted pink roses on both sides, the heel decorated with pink design. $30.00. **Right** — white slipper, 3½" x 4", with a red bow, black heel and sole, with an embossed-like design all over. $15.00.

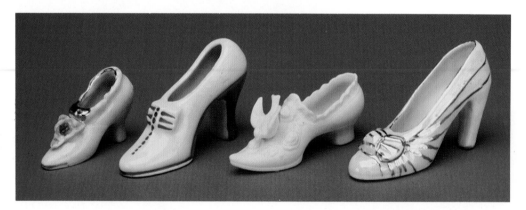

First — white porcelain slipper, 2¼" x 1¼", decorated with applied pink flowers and leaves and gilding around the top. $15.00. **Second** — white ceramic slipper, 3" x 1¾", trimmed with orange on the heel, sole, and on the bow. $25.00. **Third** — white slipper, 3" x 1", with a white bird applied on the vamp and unpainted roses as a decoration. $25.00. **Fourth** — white porcelain slipper, 3½" x 2", trimmed and decorated with gilding. $20.00.

High-heeled blue slipper, 7" x 4½", with white dots on a blue background, decorated with pink flowers and green leaves. $35.00.

Black slipper, 4" x 4½", decorated with a large red flower and an inscription on the side, "Souvenir of Long Beach Calif." $30.00.

Left — white porcelain shoe, 2" x 1½", with laces trimmed in gold. **Middle** — white porcelain men's shoe, 3" x 1⅛". **Right** — a pair of baby shoes, 2¼" x 1¼", trimmed in gold. $20.00 – 25.00 each.

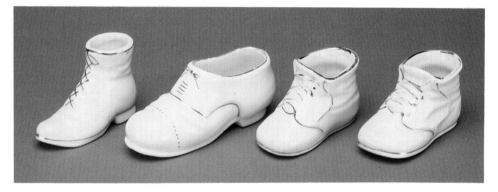

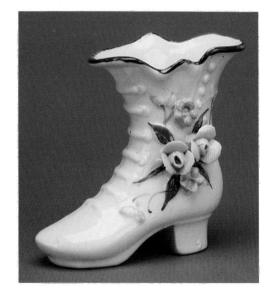

White boot, 4½" x 3", decorated with pastel flowers. $20.00.

Porcelain shoe lamp, 7" x 4", decorated with hand-painted flowers. "Made in Occupied Japan." $22.00.

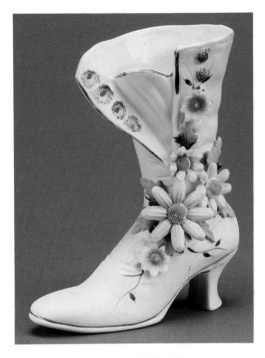

White ceramic boot, 9" x 7", decorated with pastel daisies and openings for strings. Paper label, "Lefton Japan." $20.00.

Left — a pair of white porcelain boots, 2" x 4¼", joined together and decorated with blue, silver, and gold. $35.00. **Right** — a white boot, 2" x 4", with one half painted in gold. $20.00.

First — black shoe, 3⅛" x 2¼", has a puppy on the toe, a mouse coming out of the top. $10.00. **Second** —black 4" x 2¾" shoe with a cat at the back and a mouse in the toe. $10.00. **Third** – tan shoe, 3⅛" x 2¼", with a mouse on top of the shoe. $8.00.

Left — heavy silver ceramic shoe, 3¾" x 2¼", with a large bow. $15.00. **Right** — black wedge sandal, 3" x 4½", a 1940-ish style. $18.00 – 20.00.

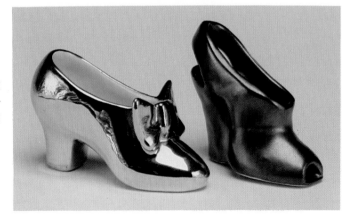

Pale green porcelain shoe, 5½" x 5½", on a wheel barrow. Decorated with fruit on the right side. $30.00 – 35.00.

Left — tan shoe, 2¾" x 2", with an animal head and flowers around the opening. $28.00. **Right** — a green shoe, 3" x 5", with a puppy sitting inside of the shoe. $15.00 – 20.00.

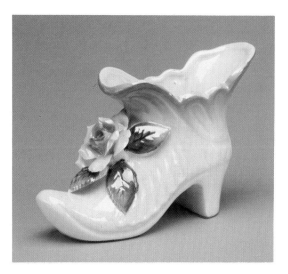

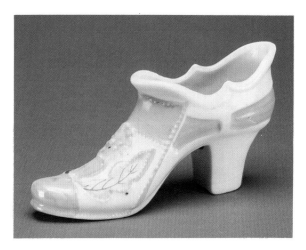

A pale pink shoe, 3" x 5", with a pink rose and darker shade of pink around the top. $15.00.

White shoe, 4" x 3", trimmed with blue across the front and back, a flower on the toe, and leaves on both sides. $20.00.

Left — teal shoe, 3½" x 3", with white dots and flowers decorating the toe and the back of the shoe. $20.00. **Middle** — beige and white shoe, 5" x 3", has a luster that is common for Japanese shoes. $25.00. **Right** — blue 2¾" x 2" luster shoe with flowers near the toe. $20.00.

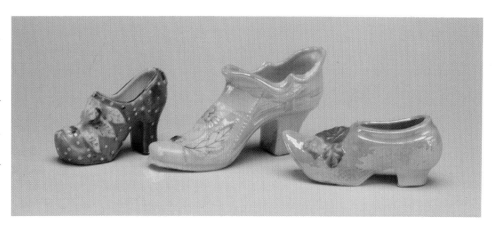

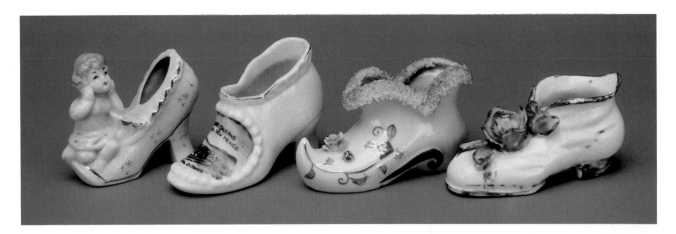

First — white shoe, 2½" x 2¼", with a cherub on the toe. $15.00. **Second** — 2¼" x 2" with a decal on the vamp. $10.00. **Third** — white slipper, 2⅛" x 1¾", with pastel flowers decorating the shoe. Marked "Made in Occupied Japan." $25.00. **Fourth** — white shoe, 2" x 1¾", with a rose as decoration. Marked "Made in Occupied Japan." $25.00.

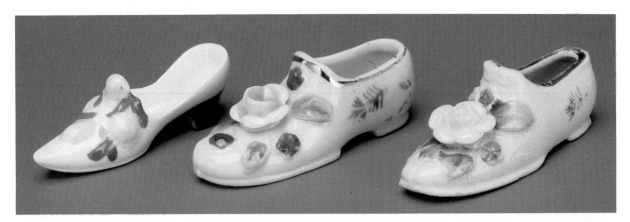

Left — white unglazed shoe, 3" x 2½", with pink flowers near the toe. **Middle** — pink shoe, 3¼" x 2¾", with a gold bunch of grapes and green leaves. **Right** — pink high shoe, 3¼" x 3½", decorated with a white flower and four pale green leaves. $20.00 – 25.00 each.

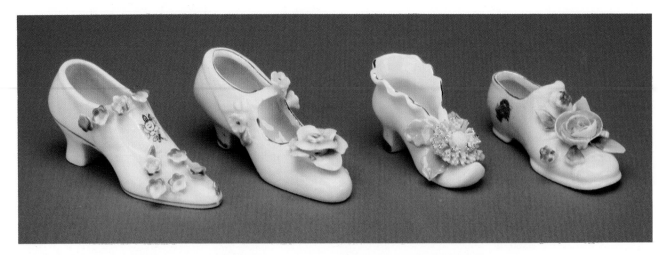

First — white porcelain shoe, 3¼" x 1¾", with pink and blue applied flowers on the right side. Circa 1960. Marked "Japan." $30.00. **Second** — white porcelain shoe, 3¼" x 1¼", with a pink flower on the front and tiny flowers on both sides. Circa 1940. $20.00. **Third** — white porcelain shoe, 2⅛" x 1¼", with a pink flower flecked with gold. Circa 1960. Marked "Japan." $20.00. **Fourth** — white shoe, 2¾" x ¾", with a pink flower on the front. Circa 1940. Marked "Japan." $20.00.

Pale porcelain pink with decorations. **Left** — 2½" x 2", with applied pink flowers. $10.00. **Middle** — 2¼" x 1¾", decorated with gold flower and green leaves. $25.00. **Right** — 2" x 2½", with white applied flowers and gilding. $20.00.

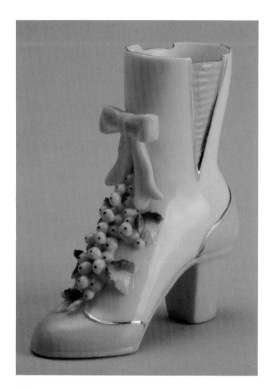

White porcelain high shoe, 3¼" x 4¼" trimmed with pink toe and heel and pink berries, green leaves, and yellow bow. Marked "Made in Japan." Circa 1920. $30.00 – 35.00.

A large 7" x 3½", hand-painted shoe with a large rose with leaves on the toe and a bow on the back. The shoe is ornately decorated. $30.00 – 35.00.

A near copy of a Royal Bayreuth without open eyelets but with painted shoelaces. Marked "Made in Japan." Circa 1930. $20.00.

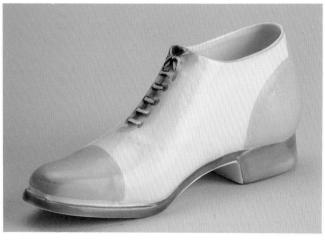

REFERENCES

PORCELAIN/POTTERY

Barrett, Richard C. *Bennington Pottery and Porcelain: A Guide to Identification.* New York: Bonanza, 1958.

Bedford, John. *Old English Lustreware.* New York: Walker, 1965.

———· *Old Worcester China.* New York: Walker, 1966.

Bohn, Henry George. *A Guide to the Knowledge of Pottery and Porcelain.* London: George Hall, 1887.

Chafers, Wm. *Collectors Handbook of Marks and Monograms on Pottery and Porcelain.* California: Broden.

Chappel, Watson J. *The Potter's Complete Book of Clay Glazes.* New York: Crystal, 1977.

Charles, Bernard. *Pottery and Porcelain, A Glossary of Terms.* New York: Hippocerne, 1974.

Cushion, John P. *Pottery and Porcelain.* New York: Hearst, 1972.

———· *German Ceramic Marks.* London: Faber and Faber. Issued by Boston Book and Art Shop, Boston, Mass, 1961.

Dreppard, Carl W. *First Reader for Antique Collectors.* New York: Garden City, 1946.

Florence, Gene. *The Collector's Encyclopedia of Occupied Japan Collectibles.* Paducah, Kentucky, Collector Books.

Gaston, Mary Frank *The Collector's Encyclopedia of Flow Blue China.* Paducah, Kentucky: Collector Books, 1983.

———· *American Bellek.* Paducah, Kentucky: Collector Books, 1984.

Godden, Geoffrey A. *The Handbook of British Pottery and Porcelain Marks.* New York: Praeger, 1968.

Haggar, Reginald. *The Concise Encyclopedia of Continental Pottery and Porcelain.* New York: Praeger, 1968.

Hamer, Frank. *The Potter's Dictionary of Materials and Techniques.* London: Putman, 1975.

Hughes, Therle. *More Small Decorative Antiques.* London: Lutterworth, 1962.

Ketchum William C. Jr. *Pottery and Porcelain.* New York: Knopf, 1983.

Klamkin, Marian. *American Patriotic and Political China.* New York: Scribner, 1973.

Kovel, Ralph & Terry. *Dictionary of Marks.* New York: Crown Books, 1953.

Lebner, Lois. *U.S. Marks on Pottery, Porcelain & Clay.* Kentucky: Collector Books, 1988.

Litchfield, Fredrick (1967). *Pottery and Porcelain.* London: Adam & Black.

Mankowitz, Wolf & Haggar, R. *The Concise Encyclopedia of English Pottery and Porcelain.* New York: Praeger, 1968.

Raines, Jean & Marvin. *A Guide to Royal Bayreuth Figurals.* New York: Raines, 1973.

Schwartz, Marvin D. *Collector's Guide to Antique American Ceramics.* New York: Doubleday, 1969.

Schwartz, Marvin D. and Wolfe, Richard. *A History of American Art Porcelain.* New York: Renaissance, 1967.

Thorn, C. Jordan. *Handbook of Old Pottery and Porcelain Marks.* New York: Tuder, 1947.

Trimble, Alberta C. *Modern Porcelain, Today's Treasures, Traditions.* New York: Harper, 1962.

Ware, George W. *German and Austrian Porcelain.* New York: Crown, 1963.

Walcha, Otto. *Meissen Porcelain.* New York: Putnam, 1981.

GLASS

Barrett, R.C. *Identification of American Art Glass Bennington Museum.* Bennington, Vermont: Bennington Museum, 1964.

Bredehoft, N.M; Fogg, G.; Maloney, F.D. *Early duncan Glassware.* Ohio: Privately produced, 1987.

Belknap, E. *Milk Glass.* New York: Crown publishers, Inc., 1959.

Dreppard, C.W. *ABC's of Old Glass.* New Jersey: Doubleday Publishers, 1949.

——— · *First Reader for Antique Collectors.* New Jersey: Garden City Books, 1946.

Florence, G. *Degenhart Glass and Paperweights.* Ohio: Degenhart Paperweight & Glass Museum Publishers, 1982.

Gardner, P.V. *The Glass of Frederick Carder.* New York: Crown Publishers, 1971.

Godden, G. *Antique Glass and China.* New Jersey: Barnes & Co, 1966.

Grehan, I. *Waterford; An Irish Art.* New York: Portfolio Press, 1881.

Haywood, H. *Antique Collecting.* New York: Hawthorn Books, 1960.

Heacock, W.; Bickenheuser, F. *Encyclopedia of Victorian Colored Pattern Glass Books, U. S. Glass From A to Z..* Ohio: Antique Publications, 1978.

Heacock, W. *Second Twenty Five Years of Fenton.* Ohio: Oval Advertising Publishers, 1980.

House, C. *Relative Values of Early American Pattern Glass.* New York: Courtman House Publisher, 1944.

Innes, L. "Novelties in Glass," *Pittsburg Glass, 1797 – 1891. A History and Guide for Collectors.* Boston: Houghban Mufflin Publishers, 1976.

Kamm, M.W. *Encyclopedia of Pattern Glass Vol. I.* New York: Century House Publishing, 1961.

——— · *An Eighth Pattern Glass Book.* Michigan: Kamm Publication, 1954.

Klamkin, M. *Collectors Guide to Depression Glass.* New York: Hawthorne Books, Inc., 1973.

——— · *The Collectors Guide to Carnival Glass.* New York: Hawthorne Books, Inc., 1976.

Krause, G. *The Years of Duncan.* Illinois: Heyworth Star Publishers, 1980.

Lattimore, C. *English Nineteenth Century Press – Moulded Glass.* London: Barrie & Jenkins Publishers, 1979.

Lee, R. W. "Specialties of the Nineteenz," *Victorian Glass .* Massachusetts: Lee Publications, 1944.

——— · *Antique Fakes and Reproductions.* Massachusetts: Lee Publications, 1950.

——— · *Early American Pressed Glass.* Massachusetts: Lee Publications, 1933.

——— · *Current Values of Antique Glass.* Massachusetts: Lee Publications, 1969.

Lewis, J.S. (MCMXXXIX). *Old Glass and How to Collect It.* England: Cobham House Publishers.

Manley, C. *Decorative Victorian Glass.* London: Von Nostrand Publishers, 1981.

Measell, J.; Smith, D. *Findlay Glass.* Ohio: Antique Publications, 1986 .

McClinton, G; McKearin, H. *A Handbook of Popular Antiques.* New York: random House Publishers, 1945.

——— · *American Glass.* New York: Crown Books, 1941.

McKearin, H.; Wilson, K. *American Bottles, Flasks and their Ancestry.* New York: Crown Books, 1978.

Peterson, A.G. *Glass Patents and Patterns.* Florida: Celery City Printing Company, 1973.

Peterson, H.L. *How Do You Know It's Old.* New York: Charles Scribner & Sons, 1975.

Revi, A.C. *American Pressed Glass and Figural Bottles.* New York: Thomas Nelson & Sons. Glassbooks, 1964.

Western World Handbook and Price Guide to Avon Collectibles. California: Western World Publishing.

Wilkinson, O.N. *Old Glass Manufacture Styles and Uses.* New York: Philosophical Library, 1968.

Wills, G. *Antique Glass for Pleasure and Investment.* New York: Drake Publishing, 1972

METAL

Bannister, Judith. *Collecting Antique Silver.* London: Concorde Books Ward Loch Ltd, 1972.

Bridgemont, Harriet; Drury, Elizabeth. *Encyclopedia of Victoriana.* New York: McMillian, 1975.

Carpenter, Charles H. Jr. *Gorham Silver.* New York: Dodd & Meade & Co., 1982.

Corbeifler, Clare Le. *European and American Snuff Boxes 1930 – 1830.* Botsford, London, 1966.

Fennimore, Donald L. *The Knopf Collectors' Guides to American antiques, Silver & Pewter.* New York: Knopf, 1984.

Kovel, Ralph and Terry. *A Dictionary of American Silver, Pewter and Silver Plate.* New York: Crown, 1961.

Rainwater, Dorothy. *Encyclopedia of American Silver Manufacturers.* Pennsylvania: Schiffer, 1986.

Zalkin, Estelle. *Zalkin's Handbook of Thimbles and Serving Implements.* First Edition. Warman, Pennsylvania, 1988.

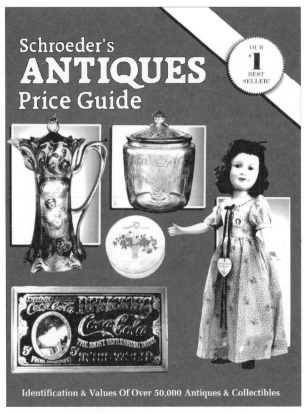